PASSIN
TO
LEAD

ADVICE FOR INSPIRATIONAL LEADERS

JULIO BRUNO

Panoma
a R^ethink Press company

First published in 2022 by
Panoma Press Ltd
www.rethinkpress.com
www.panomapress.com

Cover design and book layout by Neil Coe
Author photographs by Oz Koca

978-1-784529-76-5

To my father — teacher, painter, welder, carpenter, gardener, wine-maker, judoka, published author — who taught me the importance of being a Renaissance man.

Contents

Introduction

It is not a coincidence that I decided to write this book in the middle of the Covid-19 pandemic. Interminable hours in front of the computer screen, Zoom meetings and a feeling of cognitive dissonance with everyday life created the perfect environment for me to pause and think about my life and my long-term goals. This is part of The Great Reassessment I refer to in Chapter 8, and what better way to reassess your life than writing about what brought you to this point in the first place?

I spent my successive pandemic lockdowns in London, alone, in my flat overlooking Hyde Park. During those weeks and months, I walked that park every day, familiarising myself with its vegetation, wildlife and secrets. The park was empty, in such obvious contrast with times prior, and it gave me hours of tranquillity and self-reflection that I would have never experienced otherwise. Every cloud has a silver lining, indeed.

I became the 'squirrel whisperer', feeding the anxious rodents with walnuts in my daily walks. They love them and they had no problem climbing all over me to take the precious walnuts, almonds and pecans that I carried with me. My Instagram feed is a testament to this. This connection to nature, and the long days alone, made me think about my career, my goals and my purpose. It allowed me to be outside looking in, and I was fortunate to have the park right on my doorstep. No longer in the hamster wheel of office work routine, I was free to roam the park after a day's work. The long walks helped me appreciate life in a different way. Reassessing it was the next logical step.

At work, we had been going through a series of reorganisations, furloughs and fund raises to keep the company afloat. It had been painful, but instructive. We had to use our imagination and power through the crisis thrown upon us with drive, grit and passion, and with the utmost conviction that we were going to succeed. The paradox between the turmoil at work and the solitude at home created the perfect breeding ground for the ideas that I have put forward here.

When I first moved to Britain, people that met me would comment that I was 'passionate'. At first, I thought of it as a back-handed compliment and a bit of a stereotype: a young Spaniard 'ready to conquer the world'. Over time, I came to the realisation that my passion for life was my driving force, and I proudly owned it. The impetus to learn, be better and feel life in all its dimensions gave me strength of purpose and the stamina to accomplish almost anything. Passion, thus, is part of who I am.

This book is not a memoir, but like most leadership books, it is biographical in nature. I use my work and life experience as examples of the ideas I am putting forward. As I was writing it, I began to think that perhaps some of my experiences could be of use to someone else in the same way that other people's lives and ideas have helped me with mine. The structure of the book is not linear, but rather a series of chapters and thoughts that can be read in any order. It is up to you, the reader, how you choose to experience it. I only wish for you to find your own path, your own goals and your purpose. If this books triggers any of that in you, I will be more than satisfied. I hope you enjoy reading it. The one thing I have learnt thus far is that everyone has a different path, but we all want the same thing: happiness.

1

Your Imagination Is Your Limit

Picture your future. How do you see it? Can you see yourself there? What are you doing? How does it feel?

Years ago, I read that what a person truly wants or fears becomes their reality and it's stuck with me since. This was when I started reading about visualisation and how focusing your mind on desired outcomes was the key to achieving your goals. I always felt that it sounded too easy, perhaps a bit New Age, but when I started paying attention to my own life, I realised that I had been practising this for years. I didn't read a book about it, it was something deeper, something I felt inside: a longing, a desire to seek something more – adventure, a different life. It was the world inside my head.

As a young man I was fascinated by science fiction – Isaac Asimov being my personal discovery and favourite author – and I had a propensity for fantasy and imagining new worlds. There were other authors (Arthur C Clarke, Jules Verne, Ray Bradbury, Octavia Butler, HG Wells and Edgar Allan Poe, to name a few) that framed my childhood and adolescent years. I would include in this list *Don Quixote* by Miguel de Cervantes, not science fiction, but a rather fantastic tale, a masterpiece, that enlightened my imagination and, in time, helped me avoid tilting at windmills. Suffice to say that my imagination was well nourished at an early age, and my desire for fantasy, travel and adventure was (and still is) a constant in my life.

Picture your future

I was in my early twenties in one of my first office jobs in Madrid, at the cargo terminal of the Barajas airport. Every morning I would take the underground for thirty minutes and then a bus for twenty minutes that would leave me about a kilometre away from the office. It was a long commute that robbed me of many hours per week, but allowed me to think about my life and my future. I had time to reflect, as I would close whichever book I was reading and fantasise about what I'd read. It was a form of escapism. The more I commuted, the more my thirst for adventure kept growing inside me.

I worked exporting goods to international markets: luxury shoes from Valencia already marked with labels like Saks Fifth Avenue, white goods and food products from different Spanish regions being sent abroad. Always abroad. I would prepare the documentation, reserve space with the different international airlines, consolidate the goods as appropriate and organise their dispatch. The paperwork was all in English and that was one of the reasons I was working there. The need to speak English at a decent level was a must, and although things have changed a lot, at the time not many people spoke languages. Speaking English was my first open door to an international career and an international life.

After a few months working there, I grew restless. I wanted to do more, make more money, advance in the company and grow. I was young and ambitious and the airport terminal felt oppressive and small. Many planes were taking off constantly and going to the most far-flung places around the world, but I wasn't a passenger in any of them. I vividly remember leaving work one evening and walking towards my bus stop after a long day. I was lost in thought and musing about my life. Behind me, I could hear the roaring of a car engine, a deep growl. It was a beautiful, racing-green Ferrari Dino, and inside it was the boss of my company going home. He sounded the horn and waved at me with a smile. I waved back and saw him disappear in the distance. I stopped walking and strong emotions overcame me.

I closed my eyes and a short video played in my mind: I saw myself in a meeting room in a different country. People were sitting at a table and talking to each other. I was dressed in a sharp suit and tie and was discussing business matters, making a deal. I saw myself as the boss, representing a company and travelling around the world in business class, dressed in smart clothes and looking the part. People around the table were nodding their heads and smiling as I spoke. It was a vivid image, somewhat the stereotyped image of 'professional success' at the time. I was smiling and I looked happy. I opened my eyes and I said to myself out loud: 'This is what I want, and I'm going to get it.'

That image, that video of my future life, grew in my mind over the following weeks and months as I added more images and details to complete the original idea. That idea eventually became a strong belief. With time, it grew to almost having a life of its own. It became part of who I was, and more importantly, who I wanted to be.

A few years later, I was working in Hartford, Connecticut, representing a beverage multinational and managing Latin America, the Caribbean and the US third-party sales and distribution as its customer services manager. I had been promoted and seconded to the USA to hire, develop and train the new customer services organisation and transfer it from London. The firm was International Distillers & Vintners, part of Grand Metropolitan, now Diageo. I was not conscious of it then, but this was the beginning of that video I saw in my head at the cargo terminal. This was the beginning of an international career that eventually fulfilled, and surpassed, that dream I had as a young man.

Create a vivid image of your future in your mind. Give it form, texture, colour and depth. Now, internalise it and keep adding structure to that image until it becomes a part of you.

See it. Be it.

If you are thinking that this is too simple and that you've heard this before, you're right. I'm not trying to convey that a thought alone will make things happen as if by magic, but a thought can become a vision that will, hopefully, drive you to plan your life in a certain way. It will compel you to act and pursue that vision. Your passion and zest for life will fill in the rest. (Yes, you will also need a bit of luck.)

As a young man, my imagination was well-trained in picturing other worlds, new technologies, other realities and having an open mind. To write or understand science fiction (or fiction of any kind), you need to open yourself to new ideas and to different ways of thinking. In that exercise of envisioning a new you, you push yourself to explore beyond your current reality. If it is a certain job you want, can you see yourself doing that job? Picture your daily routine in that job. How are you dressed and presenting yourself? Are you based in your home or an office? Which city? Which country? How does it make you feel? Through visualisation, you will begin to feel you are 'it' as an increasingly clear image forms in your head. A desire takes shape, and then, inevitably, you are driven towards that desire, to that idea. Your actions have a purpose; you know what you want. You are working towards an objective – your objective, your goal. The world will conspire with you to make it happen as you strive towards it.

Dreaming about it is not enough. You need to give it shape. Perhaps you see yourself leading a company. Does that leader have studies? In what subject? A post-graduate course, perhaps? If so, then you must help your dream become a reality and pursue those studies. Does that leader speak languages? If so, how are you going to learn those? It is part of your dream, your picture, but you must work towards it. Your vision compels you to pursue this idea, and by doing so, you are beginning to make your dream a reality.

The challenge most people face is not having the imagination to dream their dreams. We tend to sabotage our dreams before they take shape by saying things like, 'That's impossible,' but if you are not capable of seeing yourself in that role, in that position, who else will believe in you?

Start with your dream and your vision. Be creative and work towards it with passion and you are already 50% there.

---

*The challenge most people face is not
having the imagination to dream their
dream. We tend to sabotage our dreams
before they take shape.*

Unfulfilled dreams... Or not

What about those unfulfilled dreams? Those that got away?
What did you want to be when you were little? What did
you imagine?

As a child, I wanted to be a Formula 1 driver. I loved
cars and engines from an early age when I was allowed
to 'work' at the garage downstairs in my home town of
Gijón in the north of Spain. The sound of the engines,
the smell of the oil and working with my hands made me
happy. I was five or six years old and loved learning new
things and the attention of my elders. I was the boy with
an endless 'why?'. I'm sure it wasn't easy to answer my
constant questions. I wanted to grow faster (literally), as
I was a late developer and my height was below average,
making me feel self-conscious at an early age. I also wanted
to be older, wiser (and taller) and be the master of my own
destiny.

Years later, when Niki Lauda, winner of the 1975 Formula
1 championship, suffered a horrific accident in 1976 and
was severely burned, I discovered my new, real-life hero.
The image of a badly-burned man racing just six weeks

after his accident and almost winning the title again (he lost it by one point) taught me a lesson of grit and passion and of overcoming impossible odds. He won the title again the following year, by then a consummate hero and my new role model.

I was four years old when Apollo 11 first landed on the Moon on 20 July 1969. Five further crewed landings were achieved, with the final landing on 11 December 1972. I was just seven and I had watched most of the landings on our black and white TV. It was difficult for me to comprehend the meaning of it all, but my father explained the importance of what I was seeing and it had a great impact at such a young age. It was like magic. What an adventure.

My favourite Christmas gift that year was a battery-operated Congost Rescate Espacial (Space Rescue). The game consisted of rescuing the three astronauts from the space capsule upon their return to Earth by manoeuvring a helicopter that went around in circles with a rope ending in a magnetic tip which caught the astronaut figurines to deposit them on a rescue boat. I would spend hours playing the game and imagining myself being an astronaut. This was one of my first dreams of a future career and life. (As a child of Spain, I'd not factored in the shortcomings of the non-existent Spanish astronaut programme at the time.)

Let's recap. So far, I wanted to be both a Formula 1 driver and an astronaut (not bad aspirations I would say), but there was also a third profession that caught my fancy as a kid. My father had been a friar (Carmelitas Calzados) and my mother a novice nun (Josefinas de la Santísima Trinidad) until ages twenty-four and twenty-five respectively. Neither had taken their final vows, but the church allowed them to pursue careers and they both became teachers. It was another era – my parents were children of the bloody Spanish Civil War (1936–39). By the time they had both left their earlier callings to the Church, they had fallen in love with each other and started a family.

We were a religious family, or a family surrounded by religion, where priests, missionaries and nuns were a staple in our home in my formative years. I was an altar boy for years in my mother's village and by the time I was ten years of age I was recruited by *Legionarios de Cristo* (Legionaries of Christ). The promise of a life dedicated to others like all those missionaries I had seen at home, travelling to exotic places and fulfilling God's desires, was too difficult to resist, and I persuaded both my parents to allow me to go. They believed I had heard the call, but were reluctant to let me go to another region of Spain (Cantabria) to a Catholic boarding school at such a tender age. I know they fought internally with their faith and their parental instincts. It could not have been an easy choice. They asked me in several ways for days why I wanted to become a priest. I thought long and hard and my last, confirming thought was: 'If I become a missionary, I cannot be a Formula 1 driver or an astronaut.' It was a reckoning, the first of my important, unfulfilled dreams. I made the decision to replace those two dreams with a new one: more powerful, more immediate perhaps and accessible to me. I had shaped the idea of being a priest more thoroughly in my mind than the other two. It felt more real and present.

I guess it took me closer to my desire for adventure and travel, and learning new things and independence. (I only stayed in the boarding school for one year, but that's another story…)

Years later, I realised that what those three dreams had in common was the opportunity to travel to faraway lands, to have my Hero's Journey. I was unaware that the bigger dream about my future life was slowly taking form in my mind. Replacing a dream with a new one is part of life, an intrinsic part of evolution. As we grow, experience the world and learn novel ideas, new dreams take shape in our minds and our hearts and we leave other dreams behind. I reckon we all have a finite amount of passion, but I have not yet found my barrel empty.

Achievement = Fulfilment

Caminante son tus huellas
El camino y nada más;
Caminante no hay camino,
Se hace camino al andar.
Al andar se hace el camino,
Y al volver la vista atrás
Se ve la senda que nunca
Se ha de volver a pisar.
Caminante no hay camino
Sino estelas en la mar.

Antonio Machado, 1875–1939[1]

Walker, your footprints
Are the path and nothing more;
Walker, there's no path,
The path is made as you walk.
As you walk you make the path,
And looking back
The trail emerges that never
Should be walked on again.
Walker, there's no path,
But wakes in the sea.

Translation by Julio Bruno

---

1   A Machado, *Proverbios y Cantares: Campos de Castilla* (independently published, 2020)

This poem by Antonio Machado has been a leitmotif of mine. Life is but a path that you create as you go along, adding experiences and learnings along the way. Nothing is predetermined; you create your own future – as the *homo viator*, always travelling in an endless trip of self-knowledge, like *Don Quixote* or Homer's *The Odyssey*.

The truth is that you never really arrive. With every step, every experience, you create a new pathway that may take you into a new direction. In the act of choosing one thing, you are 'unchoosing' another. This has been a constant in my life: going from country to country, from company to company, striving for greatness (whatever greatness meant for me at the time).

That hunger for achieving the dream has kept me going. It is only at times when I could not imagine a clear path that I have got stuck in my progress. Without a clear vision, I could not summon the strength to do anything worthwhile. I would let myself aimlessly float with the stream. Visualising what you want is fundamental if you are to get there – whatever 'there' may be.

The challenge is also to stop and smell the roses and enjoy your life along the way. In the act of always hustling for something new, something 'more', you can lose yourself in an endless search for nothing, where the goal is not the goal itself but getting there, whatever there is.

Many years ago, I lived between Paris and Madrid. Madrid was already my city, but Paris was a new experience. I had a beautiful apartment in the 16th arrondissement in the French capital. My work demanded that I commuted between the two cities and also the HQ in London. I felt a bit like the movie stereotype living the jet-setter life (minus the jet). Every morning, I would drive to work, passing through the centre of Paris, overlooking the Tour Eiffel from Place du Trocadero, taking Avenue Kleber to the famous and somewhat chaotic Arc de Triomphe (I learnt to drive it like the Parisians do: with no fear) and the Avenue des Champs-Elysées, passing Place de la Concorde onto Rue de Rivoli and then a few miles to my final destination. That drive through the utter beauty of Paris was always mesmerising. I did not mind the traffic – I was in Paris and living like a true Parisian. Every morning, I would repeat a personal mantra in my head: 'You are so lucky, you are a privileged person, don't forget that. Millions of people would give anything to be here just once in their lifetime and you are actually living here. This is the Dream. You've made it.'

The self-awareness in those moments each morning was bliss. An instant to acknowledge the reality of the life I was living and not to let it go to waste. Enjoying the moment became part of my life and it is something I keep reminding myself of, whether I am in New York, London, Singapore or Madrid.

I have met people in my career that did everything 'for their retirement', but by that time, they were too old or unfit or jaded to enjoy the things that they could have easily enjoyed years earlier. They never allowed themselves time to enjoy their present. Their drug was to achieve new things, never allowing themselves time to actually enjoy them. This is a lesson we all must undertake. As we make our own paths to follow our vision, let's not forget to recognise when we are living that vision. Don't get blindsided by the path.

The truth is that you never really arrive, as with every step and every experience you create a new pathway that may take you into a new direction. In the act of choosing one thing, you 'unchoose' another.

2

Plan, Plan And Plan Again

Most of us have heard the adage 'Hope for the best, plan for the worst.' No matter what your best laid plans are, at some point the 'worst' will happen. How do you prepare for that?

Early in my career I had the opportunity to work with a great executive with a lot of international experience. We used to talk about business on the phone (we were continents apart and Zoom was not even an idea at the time). One day, I was discussing my career choices with him. I was in my late twenties and restless. He proceeded to give me the advice that graces the title of this chapter: 'Julio, you must plan, plan and plan again.' It sounded a bit boring to me coming from a man driven by intuition, passion and bouts of creativity. He explained to me that without planning anything in life, I wouldn't be able to know if I had gotten there and be able to enjoy it. I also wouldn't know if I had deviated from my plan if I had none to start with.

He encouraged me to put pen to paper and write both my career plan and my life plan: Where did I see myself as an executive, and in life? What vision did I have? What was my plan to get there? What choices did I need to make? Were there studies to take, skills to master or people to meet? 'Plan it!' he said.

You need to get to know your plan intimately, so that when you deviate from it due to unforeseen circumstances or life itself, you are able to adapt it. Your plan is alive and it evolves with time and life itself. Putting your thoughts down on paper makes it more real and it adds another sense to your perception and memory. It is similar to when you were a student and you were preparing for an exam: writing the lesson down in your own words is a good way to remember it. It fixes the knowledge in place somehow.

Human beings plan most things. We plan for a family, a new house, a holiday or a car. We sit down and talk about the pros and cons and calculate costs, time, etc, but when it comes to our career, we often just go with the flow. Planning is essential to everything important we do. When I joined Time Out in 2015, first as Executive Chairman and then as its CEO, there was no clear plan. The company needed a new direction and lease of life. My plan was to transform Time Out and make it profitable so we could go on to new and bigger things, diversification, acquisitions, etc. But that's another story...

It was hard work and an incredible ride: the people, the mission, the evolution of the brand and the passion. It had it all. By the end of 2019, both Time Out Media and Time Out Market divisions generated positive EBITDA contributions to the Group in the second half of 2019, and we had a clear path for growth and global expansion and a board happy with the results and the overall company direction. My plan had worked thus far. Then something no-one had planned for happened: Covid-19.

I cannot begin to describe the feelings and the hole in the pit of our stomachs that we all felt. It was like looking down over the precipice. With a company called Time Out dedicated to reviewing and recommending the best things to do in a city, as well as owning and operating a series of food halls around the world (Time Out Markets), it is easy to imagine what I felt – we all felt – from a business point of view. How can you continue to operate a company dedicated to the '*out*' when everyone around the world was '*in*' and most places were closed: restaurants, cinemas, theatres, concerts, art galleries, museums, attractions and all events? It felt as if a ton of bricks had been thrown on my shoulders and those of my management team. 'How can we remain open? What is the purpose of this company now? How do we survive?' These were the type of questions we asked ourselves. Our plan did not cover it. I would venture nobody's plan covered anything like a global pandemic of this devastating magnitude. There were no blueprints for this. We not only needed to adapt – we needed a new, bold plan.

Human beings plan most things: we plan for a family, a new house, a holiday or a car. We sit down and talk about the pros and cons and calculate costs, time, etc, but when it comes to our career, often we just go with the flow. Planning is essential to everything important we do.

Plan for the worst

When I look back at that moment in March 2020 when everything we had built had almost been made nonsense overnight, I still wonder how we did it. The odds were clearly against us. We were a company whose purpose was to get people out and about in the cities of the world. Those cities were in lockdown with nowhere to go. The world as we knew it had closed down.

Our teams in Singapore and Hong Kong had already been in lockdown during February. They were working from home, but could not give us any indication about the potential spread or seriousness of the virus at that stage. We were all aware of Covid-19 by then, but in the main, we thought that (like prior viruses such as H1N1 or SARS) it would be confined to a region and eventually die out before becoming a true pandemic. That was certainly the hope in the West. We did not have cases in Europe or the USA, or rather, barely a handful of cases. Many at the time were openly saying that Covid would die out in few weeks. Wishful thinking.

The World Health Organization (WHO) declared the 2019 Novel Coronavirus a 'public health emergency of international concern' on 30 January 2020, but they did not declare it a pandemic until 11 March 2020.[2] The world was waiting and hoping.

During February, I had a discussion with the global editor, Caroline McGuinn, about launching a 'Time In' section inside the magazine and on the web for Hong Kong and Singapore and potentially any places that could enter a lockdown. There was no pandemic yet, so we were trying to resolve what we thought was a localised problem in Asia. We would talk about TV movies, online education and other similar things to do from home. We thought that this would be just a section, not the totality of the web and mag, but the reality caught up with us fast as more cities started to declare lockdowns soon after our meeting.

On 11 March 2020, the official start of the global pandemic (a Wednesday), the general manager of Time Out Spain, Eduard Voltas, called to let me know that both Madrid and Barcelona were entering into a mandatory lockdown the following Saturday and that the weekly magazine could not be distributed in the streets as usual. We talked about the consequences for the company and all our colleagues and the advertising revenue that we would lose. I burst out: 'If we can't go out with the magazine, we can't be called Time Out, but Time *In*.' The idea had been running

---

2   WHO (2020) 'WHO Director-General's opening remarks at the media briefing on COVID-19 on 11 March', World Health Organization. Available at: www.who.int/director-general/speeches/detail/who-director-general-s-opening-remarks-at-the-media-briefing-on-covid-19---11-march-2020

through my head since an earlier meeting with my editor-in-chief, but also with a friend of mine, Miguel Sebastián (ex-Minister of Industry, Trade and Tourism of Spain). He had shared the idea of being called Time In with me during a telephone conversation. He felt that there would be a need for people to do something at home if we were going to be in a lockdown and that Time Out could help entertain people globally in the days and weeks ahead. Miguel was one of the few people who'd been raising the alert about the pandemic risk since February 2020 and he was also a big proponent of lockdown as the only feasible solution in the short run. When your intuition is supported by other people's thoughts, you need to listen, and I did.

My mind was racing as I continued my conversation with Eduard. I could see the magazine going digital-only globally and a new logo was taking shape in my head. I asked Eduard if his design team could draw it for me. I recorded a video clip with my phone of a basic drawing of the Time Out logo with the 'Out' crossed off and an 'In' added at the end, like someone was changing the logo by hand (akin to graffiti on a city wall). It was no Banksy, but it was good enough for the idea. The designer in Barcelona did a great job and the design team in London and New York finalised it. I was happy with it, but that was only the start – the shell. What about the content?

The Time Out magazine team in London were a bit more sceptical to start with, as they were working on the following week's print edition of the magazine for Tuesday 17 March (St. Patrick's Day). London had not yet declared a lockdown. Boris Johnson was more sceptical than most and the UK lockdown only legally started on 26 March. It took me a while to convince both teams in London and New York to print what would be the last printed magazine before lockdown with the new 'Time In' logo. Not everyone was yet convinced that this was the right strategy: putting out a magazine with the Time In logo was the opposite of what we had been about since 1968: advising people where to go out in the city. It took a bit of persuasion on my part and we needed to be fast as we had just a couple of days to make the change and explain it to the readers. The editorial page of the London magazine on 17 March, written by Joe Mackertich, London editor, read as follows:

> 'And finally, we've altered our logo to reflect the current rather bizarre circumstances. Usually all we do is bang on about going out, but judging by the empty restaurants and deserted pubs, not everyone is up for that at the minute. Nevertheless, whether you're self-isolating or not, Time Out is still dedicated to showing you the absolute best of this city. That will never change. Stay safe, everyone.'[3]

Ominous words. That magazine and the one in New York came out with the new logo and it was the last one for both cities for a long time. In New York, the printed magazine never returned and just the digital version was kept.

---

3   J Mackertich (2020) 'Hello London'. Available at: https://digitalarchive. timeout.com/TO_PDF_Download/Europe/UK/London/2020/March/TO_London_2572.pdf

Those early days were chaotic as governments worldwide were scrambling for answers and for a common position. We could not wait and that Friday (yes, Friday 13th) we (the leadership team and I) took the decision to send everyone home worldwide, ahead of many national lockdowns. The guidance was different for each country, but I knew we needed to act as one company and offer clarity to our colleagues and show decisive action. That weekend we also closed all the Time Out Markets worldwide and sent people home. The world looked different all of a sudden. We all had a fear of the unknown and of our own futures.

Hope for the best

The days that followed were difficult. Over 140 restaurants in the Time Out Markets had to close. Many people lost their jobs or were furloughed. At the same time, we were learning how many people were being hospitalised and tragically dying around the world. Nobody had answers, but we needed to find solutions. As the CEO, it was down to me to explain to our team what lay ahead and how we were going to tackle it. Together.

We decided to expand the plan for the 'Time In' section and dedicate the entire, now digital-only magazine to 'the best things to do from home'. From TV to online education, from podcasts to books and virtual concerts and travel, the editorial teams worldwide needed to come up with a lot of new content that was relevant to the new 'In' reality. It wasn't easy and we had also furloughed a fair number of colleagues. The finances were not working out as advertisers stopped buying ads and the Markets were closed while rents were still due. We needed to minimise costs fast, and we needed a plan.

For over fifty-two years, we'd all known what Time Out was and what it stood for, but what was the purpose of Time In? How could we explain to brands, agencies and advertisers that we were still relevant in this new, locked-down world when we were called Time *Out*? We needed to explain to the company who we were in this new reality, and what our mission was. With the Markets closed, we also needed to focus on the media division to make money for the entire company and keep the lights on for the brand.

Time In was our answer: we were going to help people globally at a time when we all needed to feel a connection with each other. More than ever, we needed information and a sense of belonging. This was during the days of the applause and recognition for care-workers. We all were scared, but we needed to keep a steady ship and tell the world how to enjoy their lockdown. Many advertisers didn't buy it, but a few did at first, and then more. As they started to understand the new purpose of the company and the new mission, they bought ads and ordered campaigns. They needed to stay connected to their audience and felt that Time Out – no, Time *In* – was a good partner with a clear purpose. Early successes in Portugal and the UK were important for the internal teams: there was a path and the plan was working.

We redesigned the web globally to have every section dedicated to home-related or 'In' content. We left 'evergreen' content but retired all other 'going out' information. We had to signpost thousands of pages of venues as they were closed and find new trends for a world not focusing on leisure. We told the world why we were proud to be Time In. Transparency was important for me, both internally and externally, and I gave many interviews explaining who we were and how we were tackling the crisis. Telling the world what we were doing allowed me to self-check that it made sense. It was also good to remain in the limelight – we could not become obsolete as a company.

At the start of March 2020, I had created a 'war-room' where the global leadership team met every weekday (via Google Hangouts) for fifteen to thirty minutes to discuss everything regarding Covid-19, people, lockdowns, furloughs and our content strategy. I would regularly post internal videos made from my home to the whole company sharing relevant news and offering a vision for the company. I needed to be visible when there was no longer an office. I needed to set the right tone and reassure people that the company was viable and that our plan was going to succeed. I knew I needed to offer continuity and some sense of normality in increasingly chaotic surroundings.

Like many other leaders globally, it was necessary to become a clear voice during the pandemic for my team when many politicians were failing to reassure us of anything. My job was not politics or health matters, but rather the future of the company and its employees. People needed to know if they were going to still have a job when all odds were against us. I had no time to wallow in any self-pity while alone at home. My team and my colleagues needed my direction, so I focused entirely on resolving a seemingly impossible problem. The leadership were with me, as well as the Board of the company, and together we found the strength to go on.

It was the spring of 2020 when the majority of people in the world felt that the crisis was almost over and it would subside by the summer, a few weeks later. We now know this did not happen. Sadly, we had several new waves of infections and lockdowns, but at the time, I felt that my plan had worked. Through a timely execution by everyone involved, we turned around a situation that was almost terminal. We had refused to allow reality to dictate our future. We had prepared for the worst and acted accordingly. During the following months we needed to adapt again and our plans had to evolve as well, so we did.

Like many other leaders globally, I had to become a clear voice during the pandemic for my team when many politicians were failing to reassure us of anything. My job was not politics or health matters, but rather the future of the company and its employees. People needed to know if they were going to still have a job when all odds were against us.

Size does not matter

Do not worry about the size of your goals. What you think is big, someone else may think is too small. Everything is relative and your own imagination is the arbiter of what is or isn't possible. Your plan can be as big or small as you want.

What is your goal? Perhaps you are dreaming of starting your own company, even though you may not yet know what type of company or in what sector. Are you thinking of becoming a CEO? Perhaps you want to go into charity. Maybe you want to be a famous writer or an influencer. Whatever the goal may be, it usually starts with an aspiration – with something you don't yet have. As we discussed earlier, this aspiration changes over time, but once you have a clear picture in your mind and in your heart, you need to start planning for it.

Start with breaking down your goal into smaller parts or tasks. These are a few questions I would start with.

EXAMPLE: I WANT TO BE A CEO

- Why?
- In what sector of the economy?
- Geography: where do I want to live and work?
- What are the relevant skills?
- Education for that particular sector?
- Personal preference and affinity with that sector?

- What leaders do I know or like in that industry?
- How did they get there? (Education/experience. Check their CVs and public bios.)
- How relevant is my current experience for that industry?
- What am I missing as a CEO? (Be realistic.)

Notice that I have not questioned your aspiration or dream, so please don't question it yourself. You are in your planning mode: your imagination is the limit at this stage. You are, in effect, brainstorming and you must give yourself permission to dream.

Next, create a list with the experience and education you believe you need. For instance, you may decide that you need an MBA or a relevant post-graduate qualification, so create the task of finding the right course and applying. This will take some research, ranging from choosing the university to the method of studying and price. And just like that, you are already on your way. You are conspiring with the world to make it happen as you have set out a clear and achievable task to attain your ultimate goal.

You may also decide that for your goal, you will need experience managing profit & loss (P&L) and your experience to date is not yet great. Perhaps you are managing a departmental budget, but not yet a full P&L. How do you get there? There are myriad intermediate steps, from controlling a divisional P&L, or even a country P&L,

to a full-blown company P&L. The ability to understand and manage the profit and loss of a department, division or country is fundamental for any CEO. This will mean finding a role that will allow you to start managing P&L, perhaps in a smaller company or a department of a larger company. Can you do that in your current organisation? If not, where? How will you position yourself so that you can get that experience internally or externally? This is another task, or series of tasks, that start building up the puzzle of you – the future CEO.

As you break down your final goal into smaller, achievable and measurable tasks, you will get a sense of achievement as you complete said tasks that will reinforce your overall plan.

———————

You are conspiring with the world to make it happen as you have set out a clear and achievable task to attain your ultimate goal.

———————

Intuition vs analysis

We live in a world of data. In our digital age, everything we do, consume or interact with is defined and measured and added to the growing pool of data. The digital revolution has brought with it an insatiable hunger for data. Even your coffee machine collects data. Artificial Intelligence (AI), machine learning, algorithms… We all hear these words constantly, and more so in the corporate environment. Data & Analytics departments have become the norm, and managing a department, division or the whole company successfully relies on good data. The problem is to understand how much data is really needed and what the correct data is for any given challenge.

I have met a number of corporate leaders that will not do anything without the relevant data being presented to them daily. This is expected, and probably right, but problems can arise when data alone is the basis of your decision-making. At some point in my career, I thought that the God of Data was the answer to everything. If the data showed it, that was enough for me. The issue with relying solely on naked data is that you are then relying on what data was asked for specifically, versus what was extracted. Your query may be biased by the person who processed it in the first place as they use their own experience and common sense to ask for it. What you get is an interpretation of data sets that can be manipulated, and thus misinterpreted, depending on the person and the circumstances of the query in the first place. In other words, data for data's sake is not a good answer.

On the other side of the spectrum, you have intuition, or 'the ability to understand something instinctively, without the need for conscious reasoning.'[4] I have always been an intuitive type and have often relied on my 'gut feeling' to make decisions, but I have also always known that this was

---

4   Definition of 'intuition' from lexico.com

not enough. (Note: If you have never done your 'Myers-Briggs type indicator' based on Carl Jung's theories on psychological types, I strongly recommend it: www.myersbriggs.org).

In the middle of these two different ways of understanding information and making decisions I would argue that there is *experience*, understood as 'the knowledge or skill acquired by a period of practical experience of something, especially that gained in a particular profession.'[5] As you grow in your career and you gain experience, you realise that absorbing information rapidly and extracting knowledge from it is a valuable skill. With so much data available everywhere, there is a serious risk of getting into 'analysis paralysis' where you don't make a decision as you are unsure of the data and tend to overanalyse problems. I have experienced this problem in many companies at some point. It usually stems from fear of making a mistake. You can always 'blame' supporting data if something goes wrong, but if you don't have sufficient or clear data you need to rely on your experience. This is where I have seen many leaders fail.

We live in a fast world where decisions have to be taken constantly. Algorithms decide in milliseconds what stock to buy or sell based on humongous sets of data. AI goes through that data and makes a decision über-fast. The same applies in companies. Data departments have become not only the norm, but crucial parts of the digital

---

5   Definition of 'experience' from lexico.com

economy. Human beings don't work at that speed, and if you try to make decisions based only on available data, I believe you lose out in the long term. Unless you prefer to have AI in charge of a company, there are other factors to consider when making decisions (although maybe that's the direction we are going in anyway).

In my experience, data alone is not sufficient to make meaningful decisions. As a leader you are paid to make decisions and live with them. The company pays you for your experience, not for your ability to compete with AI (on numbers alone, you will always lose). A different matter is to choose what decisions you will make for the company as a leader, and what decisions you can leave with your data and analytics team to automate.

Every plan starts with a vision, an idea you want to elaborate, and an outcome you expect. Plans do evolve and change. Circumstances may force you to reconsider your plans or scrap them altogether. Your ability to adapt will be key to achieve your goals. One thing we learnt through the Covid-19 pandemic was that our lives are fragile and that everything we have built can disappear in an instant. We also learnt that human intuition allows us to see solutions where we have no data to use and no prior experience to call upon. We plan and replan, but must be ready to act fast and drop those plans at a moment's notice.

Through our intuition, we can find creative answers to complex problems where no data can help us. You should not be a slave to your plans when they are no longer viable.

Create new ones and trust your instincts. A new roadmap reflecting the changing reality is the only way.

———————————

Every plan starts with a vision, an idea you want to elaborate, and an outcome you expect.

———————————

3

Diversity & Inclusion: Be Whoever You Want To Be

Diversity and inclusion (D&I) are two words that we have all been hearing more often in the last few years, particularly in corporate settings. Often, a third word is added: equity. It is like the world is waking up to the reality of who we are as a species. D&I has been on the agenda for a long time, but companies are only recently taking notice publicly.

I'll start at the conclusion: *diverse and inclusive companies are better and more successful companies.* Easy. So why are so many companies globally still paying lip service to this? I have a theory. It is a white, heterosexual, male world. This is gradually changing, but old habits die hard. I am not an expert, and this is a complex issue, but I believe we mostly know how we got here and how many 'non-traditional' groups of people have been fighting for basic human rights for decades, if not centuries. From the Suffragette movement to the Equal Rights movement, from the Civil Rights movement to the LGBT+ Rights movement and newer movements such as 'Me Too' and 'Black Lives Matter', the reality is that humankind has been fighting for equality forever.

It is a white, heterosexual, male world. This is gradually changing, but old habits die hard.

Speak up

I moved to London from Spain in my twenties. I did not know anyone in the UK and had no support system. I just wanted to continue my quest, my vision of becoming a global CEO, and had concluded that Spain was too small for my lofty goals. The UK was different from Spain (and more so in the early nineties). There was no café culture or people drinking in the streets, pubs closed at 10.30pm and weren't even open on Sunday afternoons (a remnant of the First World War). There were not many fancy, modern restaurants and there wasn't even a lottery. It really was a different era, but the economy was much bigger and the corporate culture was different too. Early on, I discovered meritocracy as opposed to the hierarchical organisational structures pervasive in Spain at the time.

In my first year, I had the opportunity to work at International Distillers & Vintners (IDV, today Diageo) in a new division for international markets. We were a handful of people who spoke other languages besides English and most of us were foreigners. You could tell we were a bit different from the rest at HQ, where the majority of employees appeared to be Oxbridge types. We were louder, younger, more 'international' and hungrier than the rest. We experienced Britain as foreigners (mainly Europeans) and we were exporting British goods to the rest of the world (in my case, Latin America). I had a wonderful time. The company invested in its people, training and education and offered promotions based on results. The brands we sold were great and we loved them.

At the time you could still smoke in the office, but being quite a progressive company, IDV had a dedicated smokers' room just outside the company restaurant. The room was an interesting networking place where I got to meet colleagues from all departments (I was still a smoker at the time but I quit soon after). Clearly the views expressed by people there had nothing to do with the company itself, so let this be a disclaimer. One day the topic of the conversation was about my origins. I guess with my accent, it was a logical thing to ask where I was from. I was always eager to talk about Asturias, in the north of Spain. Unlike the local stereotype of bullfighters and flamenco, I could talk with pride about bagpipes, Asturian cider and Celtic music typical of my region. This was met with scepticism as I would not conform to the tourist image that most people in the room had of Spain, which was basically Andalucia or the islands.

The conversation continued for a while and eventually morphed into a discussion about race. The gist of it was that my British interlocutor decided that I was not white, and the rest of the people in the conversation seemed to agree. I have always identified as white, but they seemed to think that this was relative and that there were many 'shades' of white. That this discussion was possible in a corporate setting tells you how much things have changed since. I had never been confronted with this in my life before and I did not understand their reasoning. Basically, my hair was darker and my eyes were hazel brown. I remember putting my arms against theirs to show that I was as white as they were. Their reply was, 'You have olive skin.' Shades of white.

That was a first for me, and it bothered me, because what they were telling me was not only that I was a foreigner (which I was), but that I was different as well – another race. The implication was that they 'accepted' me, but perhaps not as an equal. This was all said with smiles as they tried to 'educate' me, but it really got under my skin. I protested that, in the main, Spain was a white country like the rest of Europe and that there are people of different races everywhere, but to decide that a country itself denotes race was reductive. I also did not know of a race of 'olive skinned' people.

The conversation ended that day by agreeing to disagree, but there were several more conversations in the following weeks where I tried to argue my 'whiteness' (to the bemusement of my British counterparts). That episode has remained with me since. It was the first time in my life that

I had thought about race in such a personal way, given my upbringing in a mainly monochromatic region of Spain where I'd had almost no exposure to other races at the time. This first lesson on race was probably not the best one, but it made me aware early on that this was something I needed to educate myself on.

Many years later, while working for a multinational in the USA, I had a similar, unwanted discussion about my race. This time the consensus from my white American counterparts was that I was 'Latino', not white. I laughed it off and told them to google the US Census information on race:

> 'The U.S. Census Bureau must adhere to the 1997 Office of Management and Budget (OMB) standards on race and ethnicity which guide the Census Bureau in classifying written responses to the race question: White – A person having origins in any of the original peoples of Europe, the Middle East, or North Africa.'[6]

As it transpires, I had done my homework, but the fact that this was still a discussion kept bothering me. It didn't matter what I thought, their perceptions were still based on the basis of the race they had chosen for me, rather than accepting me for who I was without any extra label. Why did this matter? Why were my race or ethnicity subject to discussion? I sought to educate them, but I realised there

---

6   'About the topic of race', United States Census Bureau. Available at:
www.census.gov/topics/population/race/about.html

was no point. Their thoughts and perceptions were their own, but this did make me more vigilant and reflective about my own choices as a leader. Timidly at first, and more as I became more experienced and self-assured, I started to become an advocate for minorities. (I had never considered myself one per se, despite being part of the LGBT+ community.) But that's another story…

As a leader, and ultimately as CEO, you have the responsibility to represent and be an advocate for everyone in all parts of your organisation. As plenty of studies have repeatedly shown, this will make for a better and more successful company.[7] My own experience is just a footnote as I have never endured the discrimination that minorities suffer daily around the world. I cannot even begin to put myself in their place, but those discussions made me pause and think about the issue in a more personal way and allowed me to be more aware of the social injustices around me. Making the case for a diverse and inclusive organisation means you need to work to achieve it. It won't happen on its own, that I guarantee.

In our professional lives, when we are recruiting, we tend to look for people like ourselves. It is natural, and perhaps easier. Together with your head of HR, you need to take a hard look at your organisation and decide if the demographics reflect the society you live in, the values that you want to portray, and if they are fair. In every organisation I have worked for, I have always recruited

---

7   S Dixon-Fyle et al (2020) 'Diversity wins: How inclusion matters', McKinsey & Company. Available at: www.mckinsey.com/featured-insights/diversity-and-inclusion/diversity-wins-how-inclusion-matters

like this and developed policies to facilitate diversity and inclusion. At the start of my career, the largest gap I saw had to do with gender. I tended to join teams where the majority, if not all, of the leaders were white men. By the time I had done my tenure there, there were at least the same number of women leaders as men in my teams. As my experience grew and I learnt more about the issues, I started to look for a fairer representation of society as a whole. Diverse companies are better companies.

As a leader, and ultimately as CEO, you have the responsibility to represent and be an advocate for everyone in all parts of your organisation.

Representation matters

As my roles grew in responsibility, so did my thinking and experience, and I would always try to reflect society by finding the best candidates, making sure that we had a good balance of international, diverse people that would add their quality to the talent pool of the company. Representation matters, and this is a crucial reason to spend time finding the best candidates everywhere. Employees see this, feel this, and are prouder of their company when they know it is a fairer, more equitable company. It is also a fantastic retention tool, because people want to work for companies that care.

In my latest gig as CEO, I made sure that D&I were part of our recruitment policies, promotions and the general culture of the company. I personally managed this aspect of the company culture as I needed to show by example. Together with the HR director, I wrote the recruitment policy and the D&I pledge still visible on the company's website.

As a leader in your company, think about your responsibility for policy-making and how you set the tone of the company. Besides doing this internally, I recommend you also do this externally. You have a voice: speak up. The famous Roman proverb says: 'You must not only be honest, but be seen to be honest.' You know you are working towards a better, more inclusive company, but how do your employees and the wider world know this? I recommend transparency and advocacy. When you talk to recruiters and candidates or at public engagements, bring up the things you are doing in your organisation and why. Lead by example. Be vocal. It will attract more people to your cause and an ecosystem will soon emerge – one that will go a long way to achieve your vision of a fairer, more inclusive and diverse organisation.

One thing I have learnt is that the work never ends. This is not a check-box exercise, but a personal belief and commitment that needs to be apparent throughout the organisation. You and your leadership have to live it and keep educating yourselves as the world continues to evolve. We all need to be more aware of our surroundings and our roles, large or small, to improve society as a whole.

The 'triple bottom line'

First conceived by entrepreneur and business writer John Elkington in 1994, the concept of the 'triple bottom line' is part of a sustainability model that encourages organisations to measure not only their financial performance, but also their social and environmental impact. Instead of focusing solely on the financial 'bottom line' they should focus on profit, people, and the planet.[8]

In recent years we are witnessing how younger generations (Millennials and Zoomers, in particular) are focusing their purchasing habits on more sustainable goods, with an emphasis on social awareness. The advent of social media allows them to see the world from a variety of perspectives, and these consumers are now looking for companies with a purpose and social impact. Prior generations didn't have this vast access to instant, global information (and disinformation), so organisations have never needed to consider their larger narratives in such a holistic way before. Corporations should reflect society, and as a leader, you need to think this way too. Diverse teams make better companies, as they care for each other and the impact of the company on society and the environment. Companies that think this way attract better employees, people who care more, are more passionate, and don't see the firm just as a means to an end, but as an actual part of their lives and who they are – their ethos. People today wear their

---

8   K Miller (2020) 'The Triple Bottom Line: What it is & why it's important', Harvard Business School. Available at: https://online.hbs.edu/blog/post/what-is-the-triple-bottom-line

'company brand' as a badge of honour if they feel that it represents their values. We are all looking for companies with a purpose that we can identify with. Work is part of life, and life is part of work. The lines have become blurred and which company you work for now says a lot about you. Millennials and Zoomers care about this a great deal.

There are no schools that can really teach you what a good life is, or what 'good' looks like. We grow by copying what other people do. We imitate our role models, and in doing so, we copy their lives and even their values. As we grow older and more experienced, we hopefully find our own values, what we believe in and who we are as human beings, and then share them and inspire other people in the process.

The work ethos of a company should incorporate the values that the new generations are looking for. Diversity, equity and inclusion are fundamental for them to express themselves as individuals. They want to see themselves reflected in the company they work for and also need to know that they can be accepted and celebrated as they are.

People today wear their 'company brand' as a badge of honour if they feel that a company represents their values. We are all looking for companies with a purpose that we can identify with.

Advocacy and activism

It took me many years to understand that openly sharing who I was with the wider world was an important way to advocate for diversity in the workplace. At the start of my career, I felt that it was better not to talk about myself as a gay man. I used to tell myself that, 'I didn't want to play poker showing my cards.' I thought that being good at your job was enough and that your personal life had nothing to do with work. I believe in meritocracy and never wanted to give someone pause if they were thinking about a promotion or changing jobs. You never know the prejudices of a recruiter or a new company and, yes, I feared that if they knew who I was as a person they would not accept me and perhaps refuse me the job. I believed that even being good at what I did would have not been enough in certain cases, so I kept my personal life to myself in the workplace and refrained from asking people about their own lives. I measured people only by their results and their behaviour. By compartmentalising my life between work time and personal time, I was effectively living two lives. My family and friends knew who I was and that was all that mattered to me.

Today, the lines between work and personal time are blurred. With the pervasive use of social media (where we share our lives with a wider audience) and particularly after Covid-19 and the growth of hybrid work, it became almost impossible to live in two worlds. I needed to join the dots. At some point in my career, I started to be more vocal about who I was, but I refrained from making this a 'big thing' as I thought it was a bit uncouth to talk about myself. I stopped worrying about what potential employers could think of me as a person if they knew I was gay, as my track record spoke for itself. Conversely, I did not want to 'use' my being part of the LGBT+ community as an entry card to anything when it became more mainstream and certain companies were trying to reach a 'quota', so to speak. I refused to be the poster-person for anyone, but with time, I realised that as an executive I had a bit of power to influence and change a company from within. I could fight discrimination and bigotry in all its forms, whether as an ally to other minorities or as a more vocal defender of the LGBT+ community. The step from influencing a company to influencing the wider world was a small one.

In the last few years, I have written articles, posted in my social channels and given interviews about inclusion issues in the wider community. I realised that as CEO of a global company with an important brand, my voice carried some weight and that I needed to use it. Someone I respect and value told me that there were not many 'out' CEOs globally and that people needed role models so I had to step up and be a louder advocate and a role model to others. I felt it was a tall order, but I saw the merit of it.

I understood that my initial fear and my subsequent coyness about identifying who I was as an individual needed to give way to advocacy and activism, given the many social injustices around the world. I didn't think I had been wearing a mask, but I'm sure many people did. When that figurative mask came off, I felt more free to talk, and more able to help others who, for whatever reason, felt discriminated against. I did not have a gay role model when I was growing up. I did not know any gay CEOs or leaders that could show me by example that you could be gay and a CEO (or any minority and a CEO for that matter).

What you do – your actions and your work – is what matters. You are no more, and no less, than anyone else. Because representations matter, I need to represent, warts and all, and hopefully help someone else along the way. Whether you are a member of a minority or an ally, you have a duty to the wider world and to your company. What's the point of becoming a leader if you don't use that leadership to influence and make the world a better place, one person at a time? Leaders lead, and that means leading in social causes as well. As a passionate leader, you must use your powers of influence and your position to help others, and what better way than by making your company a better, more inclusive organisation where everyone feels they have a home to express themselves as they are?

Leaders lead, and that means leading in social causes as well. Whether you are a member of a minority or an ally, you have a duty of care to the wider world and to your company.

4

Change Is Good

'Panta rhei' or 'everything flows', as the Heraclitus aphorism teaches us. Nothing in life is permanent except change, but most of us are afraid of change and we foolishly resist it. In an ever-changing world, we cannot pretend to stay put. The pace of change has accelerated so much that we now live in constant fear of what may come next. We are overwhelmed, with information (and misinformation) creating a sense of agitation inside us. In a way, we are second-guessing ourselves constantly and so we defy change. In Spain there is a popular saying: *'Virgencita que me quede como estoy'*, roughly translated as, 'Holy Mary, let me remain as I am.' We don't want to go from bad to worse (or that is our fear), so we choose immobilism as opposed to moving forward and embracing change.

Last century, many workers worldwide aspired to stay in the same job all their lives. A 'job for life' was the mantra of the post-war generation and the aspiration of most. Working for a solid corporation for life gave security to a generation that had lived through the war and knew what deprivation really meant. The only change they wanted was a sporadic promotion and/or a pay rise. Nowadays, this has completely morphed. I see workers in several industries like technology-based startups now changing jobs every two to three years (Millennials and Zoomers even more so), with the average tenure below three years and even less in tech companies like Meta, Amazon or Google.

Among the reasons cited for a short work tenure are lack of satisfaction, feeling under-appreciated, negative work culture, a need for flexibility and finding better opportunities. In other words, these people were not happy.[9] We are all familiar with the term FOMO (fear of missing out), on opportunities, social interactions or life itself. In our super-connected world, social media generates a lot of FOMO, often preventing us from enjoying what we have in front of us. There is always something else better, somewhere else. That applies to work as well.

Years ago, while working with a tech startup, a twenty-five-year-old employee approached me with her resignation. The conversation went more or less like this.

'Why do you want to leave? Are you unhappy?' I asked.

'No, I like it here – the atmosphere, my colleagues. I have no complaints,' she said.

---

9   S Landrum (2017). 'Millennials aren't afraid to change jobs and here's why', Forbes. Available at: www.forbes.com/sites/sarahlandrum/2017/11/10/millennials-arent-afraid-to-change-jobs-and-heres-why/?sh=5da0192e19a5

'Do you like where the company is going?'

'Yes, 100%.'

'Do you feel valued?'

'Yes, of course. You and everyone else is great and I am learning a lot.'

'So why do you want to leave. Is it money?'

'Not particularly. I could always earn more, of course.'

'What can we do to persuade you to stay? You're doing a great job; we like you and I believe you have a good future here.'

'I'm so sorry, there is nothing you could do. Please don't take it personally.' (I realised with amusement that I, or the company, was being fired.)

'I don't understand. Why do you want to go?'

'Well, all my college friends are already on their second or even third job. I've been here for sixteen months and I don't think I should stay that long in any one job. It's not good for my resume. I need to learn new things and explore more companies.'

'Why?' I asked.

'Because…' came the answer.

There you have it. FOMO. Our values and aspirations have changed. Where one job for life was usual, today, twelve to fifteen or more jobs in a lifespan is the new normal. Not only that, we are also seeing the development of the multi-career life. As we live longer, we get to the point that we want something new to stir up our lives – a startup, a consultancy or perhaps a radical change in career when we reach middle age. The new fear is not change itself, but not changing fast enough. Talk about the swing of the pendulum.

In our super-connected world, social media generates a lot of FOMO, often preventing us from enjoying what we have in front of us. There is always something else better, somewhere else.

Unlock your full potential

We are all multi-faceted – there are many aspects of 'you' to explore. As we embrace change, we need to discover the different components that make us who we are and then push ourselves to new boundaries that will unlock new opportunities. In a work setting, this translates as not accepting the status quo. In your quest for progress in life and following your plan, you should take every opportunity to learn something new, whether it's a new assignment, a new project or a lateral promotion. Volunteer for something new with open arms. Don't be coy and play it safe. It will get you nowhere. If you fail at something, then look at it as a great learning opportunity. Only those who do not try anything don't fail.

When I start a new project or a new job, perhaps in a new industry, I always use my ignorance as a powerful tool: 'I don't know what I don't know,' is my usual mantra. This has allowed me to ask difficult questions that perhaps people 'in the know' would not ask. The ability to see a problem from another angle is valuable. Ask without shame. What's the worst thing that can happen?

Years ago, I worked as a seed investor and advisor with a serial entrepreneur, Iñaki Berenguer. He wanted to enter a completely new industry (insurance), one in which he had no prior knowledge or experience. When I asked him why he was interested in a seemingly unsexy industry, he replied, 'Because I want to disrupt the industry, and for that, I must see it from the outside.' He also told me that to disrupt from the outside, you need to bring something new to that industry, what he called his 'competitive advantage'. In his case, this was the use of technology and data. He certainly disrupted the industry: five years later, he sold CoverWallet for close to $300 million to the giant of insurance, Aon. This was his third company after a telephony and data company and a photo-sharing one. Three completely different industries and one outstanding entrepreneur who has always embraced change as a force for good. Not only his own change of industry, but also disrupting and changing the industries themselves in the process.

I met Iñaki during a conference in Santander where we were both speakers. He had just sold his first company and I was working for TripAdvisor. We were both living in New York City at the time and we became friends. I have always marvelled at the ability of some people to create something from nothing; to start something from scratch and create magic. When he told me he was starting CoverWallet, I immediately became a seed investor as it was clear to me this was a man with a plan and the experience to carry it out, even in a completely new industry. It was a great ride and my only regret is not having invested more to start with.

In my own career I have always sought to find new companies, new industries, new projects and new countries to satisfy my thirst for learning and my passion for new challenges. In my journey to becoming a global leader, an international CEO, I knew I needed to expand my horizons and push myself forwards in many different areas if I was to be truly great. It was all part of my vision, and I seized every available opportunity or created them myself. I still do this with the companies I invest in or advise. I love learning about new industries, new ways of thinking and advancements in science and technology as a way to challenge myself. If the opportunity doesn't present itself, then you have to go and look for it. Make it your plan. Create your own luck.

Evolution vs revolution

There are two ways of dealing with change management strategically: do you need evolutionary change (gradual adjustments and progressive learning) or do you need revolutionary change (a radical transformation of the company)? The same applies to your life and career – the choice will depend on your situation. Do you need a total overhaul of who you are and of your goals? This will mean a deep change where the end result will be substantially different to what you started with. Are you ready for that?

Revolution destroys in order to change paradigms and values and then create once more. It is a disruption bomb that companies sometimes need, but for the most part, companies need evolution. Evolution creates and builds upon what is already there. You take the good of a company, let go of the bad and then build upon it with processes, people, culture, etc. Sometimes, we need to break with the old and reinvent ourselves. A sort of spring-cleaning of our lives. These are moments when you look at your plan and reassess if this is still what you want to do and if you are still on track.

Your professional life (as with your life in general) is a constant addition of learnings, experiences, disappointments and successes. All that makes you, you. We all need time to look at ourselves from the outside in order to decide where we are. Routine is powerful and it is easy to let ourselves go and be lost in the myriad of distractions around us. As with any plan, you need to check that you're where you are supposed to be according to your vision. If not, it is time for change. If something is not working, why do you keep trying? Look at it from every aspect and explore new ways to achieve what you want. Be flexible. The worst thing you can do is to procrastinate.

In Chapter 2, I talked about the pivot of Time Out to Time In. The revolution was the pandemic; it was imposed upon us and it changed our lives. The revolution was massive, and in this case, imagination, creation, speed and ruthless execution saved the day. This revolution is still being felt in our lives, from the new ways of working from home or hybrid work to the way we consume entertainment, buy goods from home or socialise with each other. It is a new world, born out of the destruction created by Covid-19. We don't yet know how many other changes will occur in our lives. Things that might ordinarily have evolved over twenty years have been accelerated during the two-year pandemic period. Both evolution and revolution push the world forward inexorably and we need to learn to adapt ourselves, as well as our companies and our workforce. Change brings new challenges, but always new opportunities. Embrace it.

Sometimes we need to break with the old and reinvent ourselves. A sort of spring-cleaning of our lives.

The plan continues

Since I was a boy and I started to watch movies, New York had a hold on my imagination and my dreams. I wanted to be there, what I perceived as the capital of the new 'Roman Empire'. Perhaps that was a bit over the top, but I wanted to be where the global action was. My first visit to New York in the mid-eighties was an eye-opener. New York was not the gentrified, clean and safe city of today. It was chaotic, dirty, dangerous, vibrant, smelly (still is) and utterly fascinating. Times Square was less Disney and more sex shops and prostitution. The East Village was not a salubrious place, but full of drugs, derelict houses and a sense of abandonment. The West Village and Tribeca were not the trendy places of today. It all felt like a different, darker and poorer city altogether. Graffiti was everywhere, crime was rampant; it wasn't a polished city, it was a rough, unforgiving city. To me, it was like being in a movie, a crime movie perhaps, but exciting in a slightly masochistic sort of way. It was the capital of the world and I loved it. I sensed I belonged there.

I'm sharing this because it was the moment I decided I wanted to work and live in New York as part of my plan. In my original vision of becoming a global CEO, travelling the world to represent the company and making deals, the city I chose to do it from was New York City, 'the city that never sleeps', the capital of the world. I got there by way of London, a fascinating city that was both in and outside Europe (and will always be, regardless of the swing of the pendulum which is now firmly in the Brexit quadrant). The foundations of my business career really started and were consolidated there and it will be intimately intertwined in my life forever.

As a young man at the time, I did not know how or when I would move to New York, but I knew I would, regardless of the complications of visas and everything else. I imagined it in my mind; I felt it inside. It was a calling. Many years later, not only had I moved to New York City, but I had also become a naturalised American citizen, and furthermore, a New Yorker. Vision accomplished.

I first moved to the USA in the mid-nineties, while I was working for Grand Metropolitan's IDV (now Diageo) at their London HQ and they promoted and seconded me to Hartford, Connecticut. I got a work visa and I stayed for a year living in West Hartford, a lovely suburb of the main city. It was a great opportunity that I sort of engineered. IDV wanted to move the Latin-American desk (customer services and distribution) to their USA headquarters in Hartford, where they had produced Smirnoff Vodka since 1938. At the time, I was managing the Latin-American desk in London and had helped with the rollout of a new system (SAP R/3) inside the company. I was good technically as a super-user, a good communicator and I spoke Spanish, so I was a good candidate to hire and train the new team to manage all of the Americas. I was also single and willing to move to the USA. When I got the promotion, I was ecstatic – I was becoming an expat. My plan was working. I still remember my first-ever company car – a rather old, second-hand Oldsmobile Cutlass Supreme with white rims. An ugly and terrible car, but I loved it because it meant that 'I had arrived'. I was living in the USA, working internationally for a global company managing an international team and had my first company car. I was thirty. Phase one of my plan was ticked.

Give yourself a promotion

How do you keep yourself motivated to achieve your goals if you feel you have already achieved them? Easy. Find new goals. As we grow, gain experience and start achieving our goals (partially or in full), it can be easy to relax and rest on your laurels. I don't want the same things today that I did twenty years ago. It is called evolution. Being self-aware implies you are conscious of your surroundings, your life and those around you. If you feel you don't want the same any longer or that hunger is gone, you need to focus on creating new goals in your life (professionally, personally or both). Be aware of what you have sacrificed to get there in the first place and then adapt. Adapt your goals to your new reality and listen to your heart.

In my career, I have felt several times that what I was doing was no longer what motivated me. I needed to grow, rekindle my passion and try something else in my quest to becoming a global CEO. Maybe I had learnt enough about operations and needed to focus on finances, or I was in one sector but wanted to try another. If my company at the time could not offer me a path to my overall goal, I would give myself a promotion. I would choose what sector, industry and role I felt I needed to go to next and I would start headhunting for the right company/role by finding the right recruiters or through connections to said companies. I never waited for someone to 'find me', I always tried to take the initiative myself.

The new role would fulfil part of my overall vision and it would include some of the new skills I understood I would need for my quest. It would also come with a better salary package. I understood early on that people at the top always make substantially more money, and that to be considered for the top roles you need to look like a player and command salaries that are closer to those positions you want to achieve. In other words, if recruiters were looking for a project manager that they would pay a salary of 100k, if you were making 50k in your current role, they would probably not consider you for that role in the first place. The pay gap is far too big and, rightly or wrongly, they would feel it was too much of a stretch for you. When I realised this, I became careful on how to choose new roles and how much I could stretch my salary aspirations. It was all part of the same idea: to be in a position where I could become a CEO. I needed to look and live the part as well as having most of the skills required for the ultimate role.

Those early career moves saw me changing industries, departments and even countries, but it all had a purpose: to achieve my ultimate professional goal of becoming a global CEO. In those early career days, I used to say (only to close friends) that I was 'a mercenary', but this was a facade to avoid telling anyone my career plan – my life plan. Perhaps I did not want them to see the extent of my ambition, or I did not want to entertain any opinion that could have derailed my inner vision. I needed the self-belief to get there, and as you have read already, I did achieve my early vision from that day walking to the bus stop of the cargo terminal at Madrid's international airport. This small-town boy became a global CEO, but to get there, many things had to happen first, and that included sacrifices, hard work, path changes and heartache, as well as a steely determination, to 'make it happen'.

Sometimes in your life, you need to be on the outside looking in. Having a helicopter view of your career is important as it allows you to take stock and see where you are at any given time. Are you following 'The' path? Are you fulfilling your vision? Are you happy with your choices? In the pursuit of happiness, you need to be certain that what you are doing is actually making you happy. Achieving your ambition cannot be to the detriment of everything else, or you will be miserable. Make sure you keep assessing your motivation and your goals among the inherent changes of your life and your personal circumstances. You are not the same person that you were twenty years ago. Things have changed and you have evolved. Your goals may have, too. This is why you need time to plan and to decide if your plan is still the right one. Do you feel the same hunger for it that you did ten years ago? If not, why? What has changed? Adapt your plan to your new, modified life vision. Recover your hunger and your passion. Then go at it with renewed drive.

Change has been a constant in my life, and when it did not naturally occur, I sought after it. It is a sensation in my soul that compels me to change something, learn something new, go somewhere, start over or evolve. It is the persistent tingling inside me that reminds me that my plan should go on and I cannot stop now. It is the pact I made with myself and the universe all those years ago: to accomplish my vision and to achieve my dream. Are you prepared to embrace change with all the uncertainties, but also opportunities, it brings? I can guarantee you that it will be good for you. When we invite change into our lives and open our doors with no qualms, we are bringing new, positive energy into our lives that will bring us progress and evolution. Don't close your door. Heraclitus was right: change *is* good.

In the pursuit of happiness, you need to be certain that what you are doing is actually making you happy.

5

The Hustle

Beware what you wish for, because you might get it. As human beings, we are often ruled by our desires, and in the confusing environment we live in with bouts of FOMO and overwhelming information attacking our senses, it is not unusual to get dizzy with flights of fancy, but we rarely feel so strongly or passionately about something that we feel compelled to pursue it to the end. In my book of life, I dreamed about becoming a leader, being economically independent and a global CEO. Having been brought up in a Spain still dealing with the remnants of dictatorship, my frame of reference did not include entrepreneurs.

I was a kid when the dictator, Franco, died in 1975. There was not an open society with free entrepreneurship, or even the concept of leadership other than military or ecclesiastic. I had learnt from my parents and from books and movies and TV, but I had no down-to-earth heroes, no role models that I could imitate or be inspired by (other than sports legends or the astronauts that went to the Moon, but those were less realistic and seemed unattainable for me).

My mother owned her own private tuition school in Gijón and she was the closest example I had of an entrepreneur (a female one at that, which was an oddity then). With the reign of Franco, women had lost the majority of rights they had as citizens of the prior Republic. Franco's regime put women's rights back to the Civil Code of 1889, which meant, for instance, that women could not work without the approval of their husbands, have their own money, own a passport or even open a bank account. They could just be mothers and obedient wives. It wasn't until after the death of the dictator and the new Constitution of 1978 that women reverted to having equal rights.

My mother told me how she was able to get an under-the-counter bank loan of 50,000 pesetas (around 300 euros at the time) from the director of the local bank in 1970. They knew my parents as a couple of good standing in society and my father was the school principal at a local school. With that money, she opened her private tuition school and become an entrepreneur, eventually making more money than my father. That was extremely entrepreneurial and a daring thing to do on my mother's part. I was almost the only kid at school whose mother had a job outside of working in the home and it made me feel special and different.

When I reflect on that time now, it feels like it was another life, almost like a black and white movie from a prior century, but that was the reality of Spain at the time. When Franco died in 1975, Spain began to reopen itself to the world with incredible hunger and force and copious amounts of passion for modernity and freedom. Spain in the eighties started to come out of its shell; economic growth was a reality and we had a lot to catch up on. In Madrid, we saw the birth of 'La Movida' – a countercultural movement in response to Franco's death – and the advent of a new democracy. I was living in that crazy Madrid of the mid- to late-eighties, and I drank from all that culture of freedom and modernity clashing with the establishment. It was the time of punk aesthetic and techno pop, of Almodóvar and Mecano, of Warhol and the New Romantics. Spain was opening itself to the world starved of modern culture and chasing global relevance, and there I was, drinking from this fountain of excitement and freedom. I was discovering myself and my international longing and ambition exploded. I had an insatiable yearning for the foreign culture I was beginning to absorb: its music, its cinema, its art and free expression. Madrid was a melting pot where you could be yourself and I was part of it.

A few years later, with Spain now part of the European Union, I moved to London, the land of Oasis and Blur, the Spice Girls and Princess Diana, Tony Blair and New Labour, *Fawlty Towers* and *Absolutely Fabulous*. I soon discovered that I loved British humour with its acerbic satire, innuendo, puns and absurdity. I reckon that my teenager years' pursuit of foreign culture that led me, among other things, to Monty Python, *The Rocky Horror Picture Show* and the *Carry On* movies were good schooling for my future life and honed my sense of humour – something I really needed in my new emigrant's life. In the pursuit of new horizons and new learnings, I became an entrepreneur of life.

You must want something badly

I always wanted to be part of a world that I respected: modern, creative, multicultural, fun and, above all, free. Spain was evolving fast in the eighties: it was noisy, irreverent, fun and yearning for progress and international validation, but it wasn't fast enough for me (always the curious man). I had to create my own world, one where I could be who I wanted to be: a citizen of the modern world.

In 1992, Spain felt like the centre of the universe: the Barcelona Olympics, the Universal Expo of Seville, Madrid was that year's Cultural Capital of Europe and it was the 5th centenary of the discovery of America by Christopher Columbus on behalf of the Spanish crown. We were all feeling so proud of our country, reclaiming what we all believed was our rightful seat at the international table, but everything that goes up tends to always come down. In Spain's case, it was a vertical dive. Soon after the drunkenness of 1992, we got the huge hangover of 1993: overspend, corruption, debt, and the international recession of the early nineties after the end of the Cold War and the oil price shock following the Iraqi invasion of Kuwait in August 1990.

In 1993, Spain had an unemployment rate of around 22% and it was a difficult place to start a new, independent life.[10] My original dream was intact, and having travelled abroad

---

10 'Spain unemployment rate 1991–2022', Macrotrends. Available at: www.macrotrends.net/countries/ESP/spain/unemployment-rate

it was clear to me that I needed to do something before it was too late. I was in my mid-twenties and I could see that the economic promise of a new Spain was fading fast. My future was not going to materialise there. I pictured my uncle Pedro, the emigrant whom I had not yet met in person by then, living a good life in Buenos Aires. As a child, my siblings and I fantasised about how our 'rich uncle' in Argentina had left his small village in Ávila as a young man to *hacer las Américas* (make his fortune in the Americas). Pedro was a distant inspiration during my formative years. I understood that I could also make a fortune elsewhere and return with the boon. This was my personal 'hero's journey' and my interpretation of an emigrant's life.

I had never thought of myself as an emigrant until then, but here I was contemplating the adventure myself. Rather than the Americas, I set my eye on the United Kingdom. The single market came into effect in 1993 after the Maastricht Treaty of 1992 was ratified and came into force with the 'Four Freedoms': free movement of goods, free movement of capital, freedom to establish and provide services and free movement of people. The last one felt like an open invitation to leave Spain and its unemployment and try a new life in a sort of a 'promised land that wasn't'. I could not yet get to the USA, my ultimate dream, so the UK was a good compromise. I was free to go, thanks to the European Union, and it felt like a land of opportunity as well. In any case, it was the promise of a great adventure and a different future, so there I went. The candour and boldness of youth.

In the pursuit of new horizons and new learnings, I became an entrepreneur of life.

Failing is part of the process

It is difficult to evaluate at any given point if you are on the right path, professionally or personally. Granted, you have a vision and an idea of where you want to be, but how do you know if you have chosen the right path? How many times have we all heard, 'If I had done this differently, I would be this or that now…'? The reality is that we don't know, because choosing a path is unchoosing others. This is where your instincts play an important role. Ask yourself: 'Is this experience adding value to my master plan, or is it a distraction?'

I have always loved learning something new. I approach any new learning with the same excitement of a child with a new toy. My father used to tell us, '*El saber no ocupa lugar.*' (One can never know too much.) In our present day, maybe this is no longer valid as we have too much of everything – information and misinformation in particular. In our case, it was my father's way of making sure we read a lot, learnt new things and asked questions. He wanted us to strive for knowledge. He loved to paraphrase the Roman poet, Juvenal: '*Mens sana in corpore sano.*' ('A healthy mind in a healthy body.') My father was a Renaissance man, learning and developing all sorts of skills and activities. He was a good teacher, an accomplished gardener, a judo sensei, a painter, a welder, an electrician and a published writer. I always tried to imitate him, and like him, I wanted to know about everything and be a jack-of-all-trades.

I'm still at it, but constant learning, like constant doing, can lead you to forget your goals. You have probably heard the expression 'busy being busy', and this is a trap we must avoid. We all have had days where we are busy, but we accomplish nothing. It is like the wheels are spinning but we are getting nowhere. The aphorism that says, 'Beware the barrenness of a busy life' has merit. Do we stop and think about what we are doing, and why? This is why your plan and your frame of reference has to be present. You must internalise your goals so that you know you are not just spinning plates and there is a method in your approach.

One of the things that stops us is fear. We fear making mistakes or we fear failure, without realising that failing is part of the process. We know we have failed when something goes wrong or not according to plan. We feel it and usually suffer the consequences, but this is when we must redirect our agenda back to our goals, to our original vision of who we want to be. Failure is a good teacher. It hurts, so we internalise the learning rapidly as we want to avoid it in the future. As we hustle in life with energy, passion and conviction, we succeed and fail along the way, but it is all part of the same journey.

One of the things that stops us is fear. We fear making a mistake or we fear failure, without realising that failing is part of the process.

Persistence, perseverance and passion

In my early career years, I was in learning mode and wanted to move fast. I would arrive first at the office and leave last. I would make connections, work hard, volunteer for new things that fitted my purpose and make sure I was always delivering results. I was in a race with myself and I wanted to finish first. Once I reached a point where I felt I had learnt the skills needed for the role I was in, I looked for advancement – either a lateral or an upward move – but consistently something with more responsibilities and lessons. Sometimes that meant an internal promotion, and it felt great to be recognised for your work and be given the opportunity to do something more. It meant they trusted you and that was an enormous validation. At other times the organisation had nothing further for me and I soon learnt that my internal clock was different to every company I worked for. I had to follow my own internal clock and nobody else's.

When I could not find the right internal move, I would look to give myself a promotion. That meant I had to put in writing what I was looking for, what I wanted to add to my skills portfolio and where I thought I could find it. I would write down all the transferable skills I could offer a new organisation and I would look for adjacent companies where I could leverage my knowledge and experience and also get a better monetary package in the process. In my vision, being economically independent was an important part of the equation, so when I changed companies, I always looked to get more responsibilities, learn new skills and make more money.

While you follow your own professional path you need to be ruthless with who you really are and what you can bring to the table. Put yourself in the frame of mind of the recruiter: study that job description, learn about the company, look at their financial results and check media for news related to the company and the sector. Take notes and build yourself a picture of that company and the challenges that they might be going through. Try to put in words how you fit into that company and into that role. By doing this, you are, in effect, writing the sales brochure of You. Then you have to become the salesperson of the product you are selling: how do you describe the product and its benefits? Why should they buy it? Why should they buy You?

A word of advice when being interviewed (and at every stage of the hiring procedure): do research on the person you are going to talk to. Get to know about them: where they studied, what their career path has been to date, their social profile, etc. It pays off to find common points of interests, but at minimum, it puts you in the right frame of mind for the interview so you will carry out a proper conversation rather than a succession of questions and answers. If you are able to understand the transaction of yourself as a product and the company as the buyer, you will be able to communicate value – your value – immediately. Recruiters and corporations appreciate this.

When I first moved to London from Spain, I was looking for a new international life, an opportunity to follow my dream while my plan was still in the making. My original vision and the ambition to succeed were still my priority, but I still did not know how to get there. I had been working for a few months in East Croydon, a suburb of London, where I shared a flat with four other people. I had never shared a flat before and it was an unusual experience for me. London was expensive and it was difficult to rent a flat on your own, but I persisted. I kept looking at job ads. In those days, *The Times* newspaper had a great job section on Thursdays and Sundays (yes, this was before the internet) and I would read every announcement with care, trying to find something better and relevant that I could do to start climbing the proverbial ladder. I did not know anyone in London, so I had no support network whatsoever. One day, I saw an ad for an international drinks company looking for Spanish speakers with export experience. It offered a £19,000 yearly salary. In 1993, that sounded like a fortune compared to the £4.35 an hour I was making as the main bingo caller in the East Croydon Top Rank bingo hall. But that's another story...

I was at Gatwick airport travelling to Spain when I saw the ad, but I didn't want to delay contact. I had a hunch. I went to the nearest telephone box (I know, I am ageing myself now) and I called the number in the ad. It was the recruitment agency. I introduced myself and was enquiring about the position when the lady at the other end of the phone said, 'I'm sorry, we're looking for people who are fluent in English as well, but thank you for calling.'

I was shocked. I was fluent in English, but clearly my foreign accent, the noise at the airport and the patchy sound from the public phone had made her think I was not a suitable candidate. I was at a loss for words for a second, and rather confounded, but the survivor in me took over. 'I'm sorry, I can't hear you well, let me call you back,' I answered. She started to say something like, 'Please do not bother,' but I hung up. I composed myself and looked for a quieter place at the airport with a public phone. A new tactic was taking place in my head. I had to speak slowly and enunciate. I had to sound more British and charming. 'Smile. She can hear it,' I thought.

I called again, but this time I tried my best fake, posh and affected accent. Above all, I talked slowly. I clenched my teeth, took a deep breath and acted. 'You can do this,' I muttered to myself. Before she could say anything (I feared she would cut me off), I blamed the prior 'silly misunderstanding' to the 'awful noise and the dreadful telephone box in this ghastly airport'. I proceeded to tell her how my English was positively fine, and not only was I bilingual, but also bi-cultural. ('How dare you?' I told myself.) I then explained why I would be 'a super candidate for the "amazing role on offer" given my international experience'. It worked, I'll have you know. I was called for an in-person meeting with her upon my return from Spain.

When we met, we hit it off immediately and we laughed off the misunderstanding. She found me charming and professional and loved my accent. I made sure I kept speaking slowly and enunciating appropriately, while also peppering my talk with some (in my mind) posh words here and there that showcased my command of the language. In other words, I paid attention to the image I was presenting. I looked the part and acted the part. Days later, I met the company, and soon after, I got the job. It was IDV (now Diageo) and it was one of the happiest days of my professional life. My plan was taking shape.

If you are able to understand the transaction of yourself as a product and the company as the buyer, you will be able to communicate value – your value – immediately.

Given the same circumstances (a foreigner outside of their comfort zone), many people would have given up on the first call when rejected and then blamed the person and xenophobia, been bitter about the whole thing and told everyone who cared to listen how unfair the world was. But I did not do that. I persisted and persevered with passion (what I call the 3Ps), because I wanted that job and I knew I could do it better than anyone else. It was part of my plan and I was not going to let it go. This was a crucial moment in my career: it taught me an important lesson of grit and the importance of never giving up.

This is why I call this chapter 'The Hustle'. Nothing comes easy to the majority of people, and while you grow in your professional life, you are hustling. You need to spend your energy on the things that help your plan, but also make you happy. Don't take no for an answer – at least not at first. A promotion validates you as a worker, but when this promotion is part of your original vision, it also validates you as a person because you are fulfilling your plan, your dream. You must develop grit and the 3Ps: Persistence, Perseverance and Passion to get there. It is a marathon, not a sprint.

THE 3PS: PERSISTENCE, PERSEVERANCE AND PASSION

1. **Persistence:** Maintaining your course of action despite opposition or challenges.

2. **Perseverance:** Continued effort in time to achieve success in something.

3. **Passion:** Intense emotion, a powerful feeling, a strong interest in something or someone.

6

Once You Stop Learning, You Start Dying

How do you become a CEO? Is there a CEO school? While there are studies and courses you can take to hone the skills of a CEO and many other relevant studies, there is no specific course you can take that graduates you as a CEO. In general, people access the CEO role through experience and promotion. There are exceptions, like entrepreneurs founding their own companies, but I will not focus on them now.

At the start of your career, it is difficult to understand how a particular company or industry works. Perhaps you are working in a department of a large company or as a team member in another and you are trying to figure out how to be the CEO of that company one day. Perhaps you feel that it is not possible, as you don't know what you don't know. How did that person get to the role? What did she sacrifice to get there? What did he study? What does it take? There are a number of attributes and qualities that will help you in your quest to being an effective leader and eventually a CEO. Let us explore a few.

The path to leadership

The first attribute that you arguably need in order to advance in your career is *curiosity*. An inquisitive mind allows us to explore other subjects and imagine new scenarios. Intellectual curiosity is fundamental if you want to be a leader of anything. Approach the subject with an open mind and with a thirst for learning. Curiosity is like a fire inside of you that propels you to want to know more and improve. It allows you to imagine new possibilities without thinking of any limits. This is the right attitude for anyone who wants to better themselves.

The second attribute is *study*. Learning about the industry sector, the role itself, the person in charge of that company. What do they do in their day-to-day activities? What do they need to be good at? By studying the role and the person, you will start building a picture in your head. These are the formative years in your career where your cognitive powers are at their best. This is the time to attend conferences and seminars, read books and biographies of leaders you like or want to emulate, watch Ted talks and similar. Follow the social media of the leader or leaders you want to learn from. What do they do; what do they talk about? Formal education is also important, as it will give you the strategic tools you will need in your career. An MBA or similar is a good route, but not essential; education is evolving rapidly and perhaps it is better to focus on courses that will give you the practical tools you need to succeed and not only the formal framework.

When I did my masters at the University of London, Birkbeck College, it allowed me to put an academic framework around my day-to-day work. It opened my mind to new possibilities and new ways of looking at a problem. It also gave me confidence in my own ability and I felt more empowered to take on new challenges and more learning opportunities. It was also a good break from work-mode. As I studied in the evenings, I was able to switch off from work and look at a problem from an academic perspective, framing the problem as a challenge and looking for answers that you would probably not think about while you were working. I am a great believer in continuous learning. The day you stop learning is the day you start dying, as Albert Einstein allegedly said.

The third attribute is to gain *experience*. It is not enough to be curious and study the role, you then need to gain the relevant experience. If you have studied the subject, you will probably know that CEOs tend to be generalists, good people managers with vision and leadership skills and strategic mindsets. They have accessed their roles through relevant experience. I would like to advance the argument that many CEOs come from two distinct functions in companies: finance, and sales and marketing. CFOs often tend to progress to the role of CEO. This is because these are professionals that understand, thoroughly and numerically, what makes a company perform. They live with, and for, numbers and can cut through the noise and distractions of daily operations. *They work from the inside out.* You may be surprised at how many current CEOs started as CFOs.

The other main function to get to a CEO role is through sales and marketing. Salespeople are focused on bringing revenue to the company, new customers and new partners. They need to perform by objectives, so their sense of urgency and growth is always present. They are rewarded based on performance and achieving objectives, which is a prerequisite for any CEO. Commercial people are also used to being the face of the company and using their marketing skills to sell the products or services that their company has to offer. This makes them great spokespeople. *They work from the outside in.* I have advanced these two main functions as a gate to the leadership of a company, but achieving the role of CEO could come from any other function and it will vary by industry. In all cases, the experience needed to be at the helm of a company includes both financial and commercial acumen and you will be well served if you include these as part of your learning process and your work experience.

The fourth attribute is *performance*. Without good results, you will probably get nowhere. As the popular saying goes: you need to 'walk the walk and talk the talk.' The results of your work will speak for themselves. When a company or a recruiter are looking for talent, they always look at how well you have performed in your career. It is important that you can demonstrate that as a result of your actions and leadership, your department has achieved x or y. It has to be traced back to you and it needs to be real. Good performance in different sectors or functions will also help your career as it creates a track record of you.

It is often said that the best predictor of success is having done it successfully before.

The final attribute is to *act the part*. You need to behave in a way that the person you want to be behaves. It is like an acting role where you play the part of the CEO. Like a method actor, you must seek to identify with the role you are portraying, including its inner motivations and emotions. I'm not saying you need to 'fake it' as that will not take you far, but rather look at it as the role of your life. As you think about the role and formulate a picture of it in your head, you will internalise your thoughts. If in your book a CEO behaves this or that way, you will end up behaving this or that way too. Look the part, walk the part, be the part. One day you will realise that you are the part.

THE PATH TO LEADERSHIP

1. **Curiosity:** The ability to open your mind, seek and imagine.
2. **Study:** Keep learning throughout your life. Read, study and improve.
3. **Experience:** Find roles that will add value to your background.

> **4. Performance:** Deliver consistently in each of your roles.
>
> **5. Act the part:** Believe in yourself and internalise the part.

Look the part, walk the part, be the part.
One day you will realise that you are the part.

I only know that I know nothing

'*Scio me nihil scire*' is often viewed as the Socratic paradox. In other words, if you are able to recognise your own ignorance, then you are wiser than most. Knowing that there is always something more that you don't know no matter how much you study or how experienced you become is humbling. Recognising this will allow you to keep learning for the rest of your life. Earlier, I discussed how curiosity is the first attribute you need to achieve your goals. When was the last time you read a book, or an article, or watched a YouTube video on something you knew nothing about just out of curiosity? That hunger for learning, that curiosity, is an incredible engine that can propel you to bigger and greater things. Being curious means that you want to know about things, perhaps things you know nothing about, and in that exploration born out of curiosity, you grow.

A few years ago, I was at a crossroads in my life. I was living in New York City and had left TripAdvisor in pursuit of new challenges and a potential return to Europe. I wasn't clear in my mind about what I wanted. I felt that I wanted to be back in Europe and closer to my family, but in my overall plan, I was at a crossroads. My vision was blurred and I was restless. I had been approached for several new jobs and some looked promising, but they did not fit with my plan. Then a friend talked to me about the Singularity University. I knew nothing about it, but I was intrigued by the Executive Programme run at NASA's Ames Research Center in Silicon Valley. It felt to me like a good moment in my career to get out of my daily worries, learn something new and take a vacation from myself. The experience was exhilarating. It challenged my thinking and allowed me to see the world and some of the big problems of humanity from a different perspective. Great teachers and fellow students made for good networking, too. We were all learning together, regardless of background and the energy was palpable. After the course, I felt reinvigorated and back on track with my plan. The act of learning had once again been the key to unlocking my life both professionally and personally in a moment of doubt.

If you are not happy with your lot, change it

Some time ago, a friend asked for my advice about her career. She had been in banking for years and was feeling a bit disgruntled with all the latest changes in the financial markets and regulations. She felt she was not going to grow as she once expected and not make the returns she once thought possible. She was in her early forties and was dreading the idea of starting over in a new industry and 'losing' her experience accumulated by many years of practice. We discussed her possibilities and how changing careers nowadays is much more common than decades ago. We not only live longer, but the expectation of staying in one company, or even industry, for life is no longer a thing. In your early forties you are still young to do whatever you really want to do, but you need time to think hard about what it is and then create your plan.

Through our regular talks, it was clear to me that she felt there was a gap in her education. She wasn't exactly sure why, but in time it become clear that an MBA would give her the mental space and learning opportunity to open her horizons, challenge her outlook on life and also give her the excuse to dedicate some time to herself without feeling guilty for quitting her current job. Around two years later and with a new, top MBA under her belt, she started a new company with a fellow student who she had worked with on a project paper for her MBA. That paper became their new company: she felt that she had the financial experience, and now the confidence, a good partner and the knowledge to go on her own rather than working for anyone else. The last time we talked, her company was raising a Series C with a valuation of $150 million. She was happy. She had taken the time to reframe her life, not just her work, and through the act of learning she was able to see a new world. Her perspective changed, and with it, her career and life plan.

The lesson is clear: if you are not happy with what you do, change it. Do not procrastinate. You need to be honest with yourself and your life plan. If your job or career is just an excuse to leave home and you don't want anything else in your work life, then this book is probably not for you. I assume that you want to better yourself and your career, and for that you need honesty and a plan based on your life goals. There will always be people cleverer than you, perhaps with a better education than you, or better connections than you, but you've got a plan and the 3Ps (persistence, perseverance and passion). With your plan, you now have 4Ps. *Keep believing in your plan.* You will probably never be completely satisfied, but that's a good sign.

THE 4PS: PERSISTENCE, PERSEVERANCE, PASSION AND PLAN

1. **Persistence:** Maintaining your course of action despite opposition or challenges.
2. **Perseverance:** Continued effort in time to achieve success in something.
3. **Passion:** Intense emotion, a powerful feeling, a strong interest in something or someone.
4. **Plan:** Imagine the future you want and put down your thoughts on paper. Without a plan you may lack direction and purpose.

Know thyself

One of the Delphic maxims carved on a column on the forecourt of the Temple of Apollo in Greece is 'Know thyself'. It is attributed to the god Apollo (the god of almost everything) and was 'popularised' by Socrates in the book, *Conversations with Socrates*. Xenophon (one of his students) explains:

> 'And isn't this obvious,' said Socrates, 'that people derive most of their benefits from knowing themselves, and most of their misfortunes from being self-deceived? Those who know themselves know what is appropriate for them and can distinguish what they can and cannot do; and, by doing what they understand, they both supply their needs and enjoy success, while, by refraining from doing things that they don't understand, they avoid making mistakes and escape misfortune.'[11]

Knowing oneself, knowing what you want, is crucial to carry out your vision. Self-honesty is fundamental if you are to move forward. If the plan is not working, you need to reassess it and check within yourself if this is still what you want. Things may have changed, your circumstances may have altered and you may be clinging to a plan that no longer fulfils your needs. Your heart is no longer in it, but you are blind to it because you are sticking to the plan like a robot, perhaps for fear of confronting yourself and

---

11   Xenophon, *Conversations of Socrates* (Penguin Classics, February 1990)

having to change. We have explored in another chapter that 'change is good'. Don't forget that. If you know that your passion is no longer there, then change. Now. You must love what you do to be great at it. If you don't love it, no matter how skilful you are at performing the job, you will not be great. You will, in effect, be mediocre, because your soul is not in it. You may be technically competent and you will be able to perform well, but you need passion to really triumph and be brilliant in anything you do. Know thyself.

Knowing oneself, knowing what you want, is crucial to carry out your vision. Self-honesty is fundamental if you are to move forward.

7

Transferable Skills, Intuition And Purpose

There are more ways than one to get to the proverbial top, and we certainly travel through many roads on our way to accomplish our ultimate goal of leadership and success. As we grow in our career, we learn new skills and hone previously acquired ones. Your bag gets fuller as you grow and it is up to you to make sure you pick up the right skills that will help you in your quest. These generalist skills are called transferable skills, or the abilities that you practise in every job regardless of function or role.

Transferable skills

Transferable skills are usually divided into 'hard skills' like coding or sales and 'soft skills' such as communication and creative thinking (see table below). You could say that hard skills are those that you learn and have a technical base, whereas soft skills are non-technical and relate to how you go about working. This is a loose definition, but it will suffice to make my point. We spend most of our formative years learning hard skills, because soft skills are much harder to teach and much more difficult to measure, but these are equally as important, if not more.

Hard Skills	Soft Skills
Degrees	Intuition
Sales	Leadership
Data analysis	Creativity
Computer proficiency	Communication
Coding ability	Problem-solving
SEO & SEM marketing	Time management
Blockchain	Teamwork
UX design	Adaptability
Web development	Networking
Accounting	Stress management
Foreign languages	Delegation
Social media management	Integrity

Transferable skills are the ones that you naturally use in every role, so even when you change careers, you are accumulating skills (hard and soft) that will allow you to open doors in other industries and functions. The more skills you add to your toolbox, the better. As we have explored in previous chapters, change is good and we should always keep learning. Everything we do in our careers is instructive and we should be conscious of what we are mastering as this will come in handy in the future.

Have you thought about your own skills? As you build your plan, it is crucial you are aware of the skills you need to succeed as a leader. Make a list and see which ones you have and which you still need to learn or master. Then find ways to acquire them, either through study, experience, or both. Sir Richard Branson, one of the most recognisable entrepreneurs in the world and founder of Virgin, talks about the importance of transferable skills when hiring for his companies:

> 'Time and time again I've seen people with a background of broad-ranging employment and skills hired for a job where they don't necessarily tick the specialist criteria boxes, but become incredibly successful by offering a new level of understanding to the role. With this in mind, we focus on hiring people with transferable skills – team players who can pitch in and help others in all sorts of situations. It's important never to underestimate the power of versatility...'[12]

In today's post-corona world, where companies worldwide are rethinking their work practices, company culture and employee loyalty, there is an opportunity to train employees with new skills that will help them make better

---

12 R Branson (2015) 'You Can't Fake Personality, Passion or Purpose', LinkedIn. Available at: www.linkedin.com/pulse/how-i-hire-you-cant-fake-personality-passion-purpose-richard-branson

contributions to their companies and feel empowered at the same time. This will help with loyalty, which, now more than ever, is a difficult quality to establish in a disconnected workforce.

Intuition

There is a soft skill that I always put at the top of my list and I would like to make a separate case for: intuition. We also call it a 'gut feeling', because it is, in reality, our second brain – the enteric nervous system that acts more or less autonomously from our brain. Intuition can be defined as:

> 'Immediate understanding, knowledge, or awareness, derived neither from perception nor from reasoning. Immediate knowledge of a concept exists when a person can apply the concept correctly but cannot state the rules of its application; this form of intuition has been shown experimentally in studies of concept formation.'[13]

Our world is full of noise. We are overwhelmed by it in the form of information, disinformation, data and all sorts of continuous stimuli. We can barely hear our own thoughts. The so-called 'knowledge (or information) economy' has replaced any other form of economy. We patent and trade intellectual capital (usually based on technology

---

13   *Oxford Reference Online*, definition for intuition, www.oxfordreference.com/
     view/10.1093/oi/authority.20110803100009392

and scientific discovery), but even human capital is now giving way to information, to chunks of data that measure everything we do and experience and ultimately direct our lives.

We are increasingly guided by Artificial Intelligence (AI) based on machine learning, where systems learn from analysing huge amounts of data (what we call 'big data') allowing machines to decide without human intervention. These scientific advances give us, among other things, self-driving cars, trucks, drones, universal language translation, personalised non-human healthcare and 3D manufacturing (from houses to complex machines and even artificial limbs), etc, but with every bit of technology advancement, we lose a part of ourselves. Knowledge is being replaced by information and disinformation, but there is no quality prerequisite to those bits of data. It is just data, and in this game, machines have a tremendous advantage. Our brains cannot process data at those impossible speeds and we are being left behind as human beings. Or are we? We have something in our toolbox that (so far) machines do not have: *intuition*.

I am certain that you have often experienced that sensation that compels you to do something (or to do nothing). Gut feelings are the manifestation of your intuition, and although they may sometimes be a projection rather than the truth, we should all pay more attention to our intuition. We started the book discussing your vision, your career, and your life plan. Your vision would have been guided by the intuition that you should do this or that in your life.

You allowed yourself to manifest the thoughts that would drive you to change and achieve overall betterment in your life. Consciously or not, you listened to your gut.

Intuition is associated with the right side of the brain, the creative side (sometimes referred to as the analogue brain). In the right side we deal with imagination, creativity, rhythm, visualisation and the arts. In the left side, or digital brain, we find our analytical and verbal skills, our logic, linear thinking and facts. Both sides of the brain are needed for us to function, but it is thanks to our right brain that we are able to visualise our future, imagine a different one and be guided there.

I had a teacher who was a great inspiration in my life. He taught me first in primary school at around six years of age, and then again when I was around ten. His name was Don Manuel Morán. One of the key tenements of his teaching methods was to use your imagination, and thus, your intuition. His classes were always different, unexpected and fun. Some days he would ask us all to change seats – whoever was sitting at the front went to the back and vice-versa, so the class had a new seating arrangement. On other days he would ask us to sit on the floor to 'change our perspective' and resolve a problem. Don Manuel would use bright colours in his teachings 'to aid with memory' and would give us gummy sweets and bright candy every time we did something right. He had a notebook where he would reward us with a *punto gordo* (big point) or a *punto flaco* (small point), depending on our achievements and behaviour in class. At the end of the year, we would exchange those points for gummies and other treats. It was healthy competition (perhaps not for our teeth) and it was fun. Don Manuel believed in the power of intuition by way of creativity and wanted to hone that skill within us. He knew that the right brain had a lot to contribute to humankind, and sadly, education in those days was not focused on teaching soft skills.

I was around ten when one day he sat us on the floor and asked us 'to use our imagination' to resolve a mathematical problem instead of using a logical mathematical equation. It was a problem about pipes and swimming pools. I let my imagination run wild. I visualised how a superhero would hold all the water in their hands while the drains were opened and then I made a simple division to get to the result. I'm not sure exactly how it went, it was such a long time ago, but I resolved it. My intuition, my gut, allowed me to positively know that it was correct, even though I wasn't sure how. It was a mini-triumph of the imagination. Don Manuel was quite theatrical and he bestowed a grand-sounding name to my solution: *el 'Método Bruno'* (the Bruno Method). That got me an A in maths for the rest of that year. I was so proud of myself, and above all, I learnt a crucial lesson: use the power of your imagination. I knew the answer was right, but I did not know why. I just knew; it was my intuition. Since then, I have made sure to listen to my intuition for the big challenges and opportunities in life.

Purpose

Intuition brings you instant knowledge without reason or logic, but you need something more in your toolkit to harness your vision, and that is purpose. Without purpose, you are like a fish aimlessly swimming with the current, rather than against it. In our world full of information and noise, we tend to focus on the short term. We achieve an immediate goal and then add more goals to keep us feeling busy and fulfilled. This stops us from really discovering our purpose in life. What do you want to achieve? Life is not happening to you: you are the one making the decisions that create your life. You must be the driver of your own life.

In my life vision, I wanted to become a global leader, to be respected and recognised by my peers and be financially independent. But why? What was my purpose? It has taken me many years to understand that besides all of the above, I sought to inspire others as I had been inspired by people close to me and by books, great books that brought me ideas and new worlds and new passions. I wanted to make money and be successful and be recognised for it and then help others to do the same. I wanted to become economically independent and self-sufficient. I longed to travel the world and experience new lives, different beliefs, meet different people, love and be loved, and learn and grow in the process. I wanted to live a fulfilling life and be happy.

Your purpose is about *who* you want to be rather than *what* you want to be. My original vision allowed me to see a future of 'what', but not a future of 'who'. Happiness is not a destination, but a path. When you find meaning and purpose in what you do rather than following a succession of immediate goals, you are on the right path. And it is the path that matters; the journey, not the destination. I am still on that journey today, learning and searching for answers. Every time I think I am closer to an answer, I find that there is another road to take, another idea to pursue or a new adventure ahead of me.

Build your career with the end in mind

Sometimes we are tempted by following the current and going with the flow to see what happens. Leaving things to fate in my opinion is not a great recipe for success. I have been arguing that planning your career and setting your own expectations is the right thing to do as you will be able to shape your decisions accordingly. This is why we discussed in Chapter 2 the need to plan, plan and plan again.

Your plan should be built from your heart by way of your head. Your intuition will help you find your calling and your purpose. The rest is up to you. As you develop your transferable skills and check your boxes, you will continue to discover new aspects of yourself that you like or even dislike. Step by step, your path will be clearer and straighter as you cut off some of the branches that take you nowhere. Above all, don't forget to enjoy yourself. Finding your purpose in life is a big task that will take you a lifetime in most cases, so enjoy the path as you make it.

——————————

You must be the driver of your own life. Happiness is not a destination, but a path. When you find meaning and purpose in what you do, rather than following a succession of immediate goals, you are on the right path.

——————————

8

We Are In This Together: A Post-pandemic World

Corporate life is tough. There are thousands of articles and books dedicated to this topic. A search in Google for 'corporate life is tough' generated 106 million results for me. I read a few of the articles and it was depressing. I have spent over thirty years in corporations and I have experienced all sorts of emotions. I've also seen how work practices have evolved throughout this time. Rapid advancements in technology allow us to be connected with global communities in ways that we never could before. We can see how other people live and work and want the same for ourselves. Information is power, and in the knowledge and information economy we are living in, employees can now demand a much bigger say on how they want to work.

The Great Reassessment

We are currently living in the midst of an economic era being referred to as 'The Great Resignation',[14] or what some people (me included) prefer to call 'The Great Reassessment'. In a post-Covid world, employees the world over are feeling disconnected to their companies and are reassessing their careers and their motivations. As we were all collectively forced to push the pause button, we had time to think about what was important in our lives and careers. We had to reassess our work conditions and our goals, and what many people felt, en masse, is that their careers were not at all what they wanted.

When companies worldwide had to furlough and lay off millions of workers, it was a true moment of clarity for many people, who asked, 'What am I doing in this company? Why am I here? What is my purpose?' We all realised our own frailty in the workplace, now compromised by the pandemic. We were not in control and we needed to regain some semblance of it. Resigning and looking for a new job or a new career was sort of an exercise in freedom. It empowered us to think about what we wanted in life. It allowed us to take an important step and move past the pandemic. We said to ourselves and to the world, 'I am in charge,' and we started over, but more conscious of our purpose and our long-term goals.

---

14 K Morgan (2021) 'The great resignation: How employers drove workers to quit', BBC.co.uk. Available at: www.bbc.com/worklife/article/20210629-the-great-resignation-how-employers-drove-workers-to-quit

Corporations need to adapt to this new way of thinking about work in the knowledge and information economy that we live in. Following the Great Recession in 2007–2009 (which began with the collapse of the US housing market coupled with lax regulation and risky behaviour in their financial markets, and then spread out around the world),[15] many companies started exploring different methods of working. It was arguably around this time that the concept of 'a job for life' finally died. Following bankruptcies and massive layoffs everywhere, employees stopped believing in corporations. The idea of company loyalty was abandoned. Some progressive companies started offering flexible working as a new perk following increased demand from the workforce, but it was a retention tool sparingly used. Many managers still believed that being in the same place, seeing the workforce in situ, was a necessity for productivity and cohesion in an organisation. Part-time work slowly became more pervasive and job sharing became possible. These new ways of working were normalised and HR departments had to adapt.

As commuting times increased and the cost of living increased in the cities, people moved to the suburbs. The Great Recession made more people decide to work for themselves, young and old, and this explosion of entrepreneurship created new ways of perceiving and living (or not) traditional corporate lives. New types of creative and collaborative leaders emerged and this accelerated these changes. However, the largest impact to

---

15   Definition of 'Great Recession', www.investopedia.com/terms/g/great-recession.asp

change in corporate culture occurred during the global pandemic of Covid-19. The move to working from home (WFH) was initially thought to be a temporary measure, but then it became the norm as intermittent lockdowns made people weary of commuting and working in an office environment. This, combined with increasing travel times and costs, made it easier at first (and almost an obligation two years later) to shift the concept of working in an office to working from home. The acronym WFH became mainstream.

Corporations started to close down or reduce headquarters and satellite offices. People were not using them for months and the high costs of maintaining empty offices became apparent on the bottom line. Why would you keep those offices if only a few people were using them? Realising that the tide was changing and employees now demanded the flexibility they never truly got ten years earlier, some tech giants started to shift their policies. A few companies also realised that they needed to use first-mover advantage and be seen as modern organisations caring for their employees. The concept of hybrid working was born, and this is only the beginning. Employees are demanding a changing work environment better suited to their lives. The pendulum has shifted.

We are living in the midst of The Great Resignation, or what some people (me included) prefer to call The Great Reassessment.

Remote technologies and the new office

I remember the late nineties and early noughties when remote working was not yet a thing. We started using audio-conferencing as a means to save costs in travel and a better use of people's time. Soon after, a few companies started working on perfecting video-conferencing. With the development of the internet, high internet speed and better technology, new services like Skype and iChat started to enter our lives, as well as corporate solutions like BlueJeans, Tandberg, Cisco, Huawei and others.

With the rapid deployment of smartphones worldwide, we started carrying our own video-conferencing facilities with us and today we can use Zoom, FaceChat, WeChat, Slack, Hangouts, Meet, WhatsApp and many other ways to video-communicate with each other from the comfort of our palms. If anything, we are now over-communicating with each other after interminable Zoom meetings at work and constant video chats with our family and friends. We are arguably suffering from over-exposure to all this technology. In fact, the problem today is how *not* to communicate constantly with everyone.

Due to the accessibility and affordability to communicate remotely and still be engaged, it is clear that hybrid work will be the favoured solution for most knowledge-based organisations. As these new patterns of work emerge, corporations will need to adapt as workers cannot yet replace the office as we know it. Homes, for most people, are not ready to become offices as well. Many people, particularly at the start and middle of their careers, do not have the extra space for a proper office, or even reliable, high-speed internet access. The tools and technology need to evolve and adapt to this new reality of millions of people working from home without the infrastructure that a corporate office affords. Work policies also need to be rewritten to reflect the new hybrid-work reality.

The future of 'office' work

Remote working is not the panacea for today's economy either. We have a clear division in society between white-collar and blue-collar workers, between the office-based employee that can easily work from home and the rest of the workforce that needs to be at the premises, from hospitality to care workers, from agriculture and manufacturing to all other types of services-based economy. These workers cannot work from home, with or without Covid-19. The sense of unfairness has been obvious throughout the pandemic and it will take years, if not decades, to resolve as the world finds new ways to work together. This social divide is going to be analysed at length, but for the purpose of this book, I will focus on the future of office work.

As we adapt to the new reality of 'living' with the endemic virus, ideas will continue to evolve. There will be some geographical and cultural differences when applying the new principles of hybrid working in the distributed workforce, but I am confident that 'office work' as we once knew it has changed for good. Yes, there is a clear divide between the white-collar vs the blue-collar workers, between the ones that can work from home and the ones that don't, and this will be important when developing new equitable policies for the workforce. As we create the workplace of tomorrow, we need to redefine its basic premises. With remote working, we need new rules as employees will no longer rely on a physical location for all their needs. Here are a few ideas about this new work reality and how it can be implemented.

THE FUTURE OF THE OFFICE

- **A distributed workforce:** The office must be location-agnostic, whether at home, at the company's premises, a co-working location or a combination of all. Employees in the knowledge-based economy will be based where it suits them both economically and personally.

- **WFH:** Homeworking must include office equipment that the corporation needs to provide and pay for: high-speed internet, adequate office essentials, software and training.

- **Productivity:** This needs to be redefined with new KPIs (Key Performance Indicators). People are no longer 100% in an office environment, so how do we measure these?

- **Meetings:** These need to be hybrid: both physical and remote at the same time. Technology needs to adapt to this.

- **Meetings overload:** Not being physically in an office cannot mean always being connected to a Zoom meeting. Employees need time to actually action things, not just be in meetings.

- **Death by email:** Email overload needs to be reduced significantly. It creates unnecessary anxiety and it has been proven to be a blunt tool.

- **Asynchronous working:** This will become the norm. Working 9–5 is dead. Office hours need a new paradigm because WFH also means keeping unusual hours, but output doesn't need to suffer because of this.

- **Virtual collaboration tools:** These allow managers and companies to understand their employees (eg, where they are spending their time, in what patterns, etc) and adapt and redirect as needed.

- **Remote leadership:** This needs to evolve as managers need to learn new skills to motivate, manage and develop a hybrid workforce. This will be part of the curriculum of business schools and HR departments alike. New leaders for a new world.

- **Test, learn and iterate:** This approach towards processes should become part of the evolution of organisations.

- **Talent acquisition:** Hiring models need to be redefined and not be location-based. This will also mean looking at salaries not tied to the cost of living in specific cities.

- **Company culture:** This should focus on the wellbeing of the workforce and will include team days at the office and team-building events, as well as regular video presentations from leadership focusing on culture, training and creating a sense of belonging.

Earlier in the book, I talked about my own experience leading Time Out during Covid. It was in March 2020 that, with the world in lockdown, the Time Out Markets closed. With everyone working from home, we needed to rethink the office situation around the world. It was an odd sensation to be paying for office space that was not being used and it also felt unfair. There was no rulebook for this situation and we needed to take action, and fast. One of the first decisions I took was not to renew the main HQ space in London and give notice in New York and other smaller offices around the world.

By June 2020, the first global lockdown had mostly passed, and for a few weeks we all felt (wrongly) that the world was returning to normality, but we were not clear on whether we needed to rent the same amount of space as before. After extensive consultation with employees and the global leadership team, we came to the conclusion that most people preferred to work from home, but would have a few 'office days'. A hybrid model. We made some calculations and started to design how this new physical office would look and what amount of space we would ideally need. We ended up with a new design that fitted a new purpose. I have summarised it here:

- Hot-desking: Everyone could reserve an actual desk for the day via an app on a first-come, first-served basis.

- Several collaborative areas open to all with sofas, chairs and a mixture of long and short tables for meetings or for working side by side.

- Everyone was given a laptop. No more desk monitors or PCs, except for the design team and IT.

- No landline telephones anywhere except at reception.

- A few meeting rooms, to be booked via the app in forty-five-minute increments.

- A small kitchen.

- Unisex bathrooms.

- Three offices to be shared by management and to be used as extra meeting rooms when not occupied by said management. That included the office of the CEO.

This change not only allowed the company substantial savings (and given the economic crisis created by the pandemic, these were really welcome), but above all, we developed a new way of working by putting the employee at its core. We decided to be pioneers and made the changes before most companies did, so we could also showcase this as a new talent acquisition and retention tool. People felt heard and respected and it was a truly win-win situation.

There were teething problems, like days when all the desks were busy and people had to work sitting on a sofa next to a coffee table, or the rare days when all the leaders were in the office and there were not enough offices for all. I heard a few complaints here and there, and to be honest, it was odd and somewhat funny at the same time. People were moaning about office space when we had gone through months of working in kitchens, bedrooms and living rooms with children, dogs and cats all around us. I was surprised at how entitled they could be about 'their' office space even in the middle of a pandemic. I remember talking to a leader in my team about the new situation – how people complained about small things and how possessive they were of their perceived space. The conclusion was that many people wanted to work from home when they chose to, and without any permission, but also expected an office space marked just for them should they decide to go to the office on any random day. (And, of course, coffee, tea, milk and other amenities as if they had never left the office in the first place.) In other words, they wanted to have it all, plus total freedom to decide what to do and when. Our expectations have certainly changed in these two years!

The trend towards flexibility of hours, flexibility of location and collaborative decision-making has now become part of the expectation rulebook of all employees and I don't see us ever going back to pre-pandemic office norms. During the two years of Covid-19 we have gone through an imposed revolution, a total disruption of existing processes and structures, and because this disruption is considered a positive one by most people, it's here to stay. We have accelerated the way we work and live by at least twenty years. We had no choice – the change was abrupt, without the need for consensus, and it was largely received with open arms.

As we return to work in a post-pandemic world, there are still many unanswered questions, but we all know that we are being part of a new global and unplanned experiment that will frame the office of the future, new work processes and our relationship with corporations and each other. One question I ponder on is what will happen with the city centres and the economy of the cities as people stay away for most of the week. What will the future of all those retail businesses that have moved almost completely online be? Will they reopen? If so, in what form? What about those sandwich shops and restaurants catering to office workers? Will they be able to survive if there are no office workers from Monday to Friday? The city is also evolving fast and the changes in real estate and taxation are going to be profound. What will the city centre be in a new world with mostly tourists and the occasional leisure visitors? Time will tell, but I hope policy-makers tackle this soon.

We are part of a new global and unplanned experiment that will frame the office of the future, new work processes and our relationship with corporations and each other.

Social awareness and social impact

After two years of working with your colleagues virtually, regardless of what country or location they were in, we have all had a shared experience of something much bigger than any of us. We felt powerless and scared, but we were united in our fear and our hopes. This also brought new opportunities as we had to expand our usual circle of collaboration exponentially. We started to see how the new reality was affecting everyone, whether they were from Asia or Europe. We found that we had many more things in common that united us rather than separated us. We discovered a common human experience in the adversity and uncertainty of the future. We got closer together. We listened more, we shared more. We opened our kitchens and living rooms to strangers from all over the world and we did not mind. Covid-19 has changed us forever.

The world shared a common goal and purpose: to get rid of Covid-19 and get the world moving again. We wanted to regain our freedom and this common purpose has brought us closer than ever. We realised that we all wanted the same, regardless of age, race, colour, disability, gender, gender identity, national origin, creed or sexual orientation. We learnt that thinking outside the box is no longer the staple proposition for thinking differently. We now prefer to have no box at all and use our imagination and creativity to resolve our problems and the problems of the world. This is an evolution that will mark us for generations to come. Now we can look at our corporate problems of old – pre-pandemic – and apply new ideas to resolve them.

Don't think outside the box,
think as if there is no box.

Corporations have always had origin stories. Brands have always had heritage; but the idea of social impact is larger than a company itself: it means a company must consider how it fits into the rest of the world and what it gives back to society. The eighties paradigm of 'bottom line' has been replaced by the 'triple bottom line': people, profits and the planet. It is no longer just about measuring business profit, but also positive social impact. This means that change begins in the boardroom and CEOs have a larger responsibility than ever before.

Given both the new consumer landscape and the information economy, we need to see businesses as a force for good – especially as a number of corporations have more sway and power than most governments in this world do, with multi-billion or even trillion valuations that dwarf dozens of countries' GDP. We have begun to witness a sea-change with respect to that bottom line. Certified B-Corps (a designation developed by a number of transnational organisations, including the United Nations) balance 'purpose and profit'. Today there are over 5,000 companies with this designation. It's not just altruistic or a 'nice thing to do', it is actually smart. Aside from being a pretty label that can draw in customers, this designation, and the bloc of companies that have it, wields political influence and clout.

These platforms allow CEOs of such companies a certain prominence on the world stage as thought leaders and pioneers. Much as companies can use the bottom line and their customer base to sway the market to awareness and to certain causes, a CEO has a chance to assert themselves in the marketplace by being a mouthpiece to advance social good without the shackles of political discourse. They are more free than politicians to make a case for good and to put their money where their mouth is.

This is important for a number of reasons. Firstly, because of the aforementioned transnational power and influence. From Google to Apple, massive corporations across the globe are wealthier than most governments and need to hold themselves accountable as such. We have already seen the fallout from when they don't – using their influence for good is particularly crucial post-Covid. During the pandemic, many CEOs stepped up to do right, such as Mary Barra, the CEO of General Motors. Forbes reported that the company 'was converting auto factories to ventilator production before most companies had even acknowledged what was about to land on their balance sheets.'[16] And it's not just Western corporations. Chinese firms Alibaba and Pinduoduo have both demonstrated their commitment to ESG (Environmental, Social and Governance). At the end of 2021, Citi raised a record-breaking US$40 billion for Asia Pacific clients' sustainable financing needs.[17] This is not a passing trend of virtue signalling – there is clearly a lot of money to be made by doing good.

---

16 E Garsten (2020) 'GM's Mary Barra offers to build ventilators for coronavirus patients at idled auto plants', Forbes. Available at: www.forbes.com/sites/edgarsten/2020/03/18/gms-barra-offers-to-build-ventilators-in-idled-plants/?sh=709b6f184754

17 No author (2021) 'Citi Sets Record For Asia Pacific Sustainable Financing', MarketScreener.com. Available at: www.marketscreener.com/quote/stock/CITIGROUP-INC-4818/news/Citi-Sets-Record-for-Asia-Pacific-Sustainable-Financing-36956342

Beyond the profit companies stand to gain by doing the right thing, business leaders must also prioritise forward thinking, as we have the unique ability to create a path that governments can follow. As much as corporations are beholden to shareholders, they have considerably more flexibility to take action compared to the slow-turning gears of bureaucracy that fetter most modern democracies. Time and again we have seen the private sector push forward progress before governments took action. In the United States, social integration, women's rights and gay rights were championed in the private sector decades before the law caught up, if it has at all. Indeed, nearly fifty years after it was first proposed in 1972, the Equal Rights Amendment still sits oddly, and sadly, unratified.

Additionally, urgently needed sustainability efforts which should concern us all regardless of political leaning are stymied by polarised politicking, while a number of Fortune 500 companies have committed to green energy by partnering with the Environmental Protection Agency (EPA) in the USA.[18] Arguably, corporations that are quick to respond to consumer 'moral and ethical concerns' generate a bigger impact on society than the gridlocked politicians they have elected. In today's world, where consumers are more attuned to issues of racial, gender and social equity, 'voting with your dollars' is just as important as voting in elections. The power of social media with the ability to cancel or shame a company has a much

---

18 'Green Power Partnership Fortune 500 Partners List', Environmental Protection Agency. Available at: https://19january2017snapshot.epa.gov/greenpower/green-power-partnership-fortune-500r-partners-list_.html

stronger and more immediate impact in society than any democratic election. Corporations cannot wait years until the next election; they must react immediately and publicly to avoid reputational damage and revenue impact.

In pushing forward progress, corporations and their CEOs play a crucial role. As the face of a corporation, the CEO sets the tone for company culture, adapts to changing circumstances and reacts rapidly to the needs of the consumer and society at large. Leaders who set examples with their own behaviour encourage good corporate governance and can pass on their ideas and beliefs not just to their own organisation, but to the larger economy in meaningful, impactful ways. If indeed we are in this together, it is up to all of us to make sure that as we change ourselves, we also change our planet for the better.

How do you behave in your own company and team? Are you adopting new and better ways of working adapted to the new reality? Do you involve your colleagues in the decision-making that involves their wellbeing and how they work with each other? The Great Reassessment is pushing people to gain clarity about their work-life balance more than ever before. How will you adapt to this new world?

In today's world, where consumers are more attuned to issues of racial, gender and social equity, 'voting with your dollars' is just as important as voting in elections.

9

Triumph And Disaster: Two Impostors

If you can dream – and not make dreams your master;

If you can think – and not make thoughts your aim;

If you can meet with Triumph and Disaster

And treat those two impostors just the same

R Kipling

This is a fragment of the most popular poem by Rudyard Kipling, 'If'. It was published in 1910, but to me, it feels current. This part of the poem has always resonated strongly with me. It teaches me that circumstances change and external factors (good and bad) are unpredictable and, of course, relative. You must do whatever is needed at any particular time and the rest will follow. You are neither success nor failure, as both are external to you. You are you. Who judges what success is? Who decides it? Is it important? Usually, we tend to measure success by the views of other people, and it is the same regarding failure. What we accept as conventional wisdom is highly influenced by our own upbringing. Everything is subjective.

If you look back at your professional life, how many of your decisions have been influenced by other people's perceptions? Are you living your life for them? It is impossible managing other people's expectations, so you should concentrate on knowing what you want, who you are, and then plan how to get there. What you may feel as success, someone else may see as failure. Perhaps their expectation of you was different. The stereotype of a successful career consisting of attending the 'right' university and then following a predefined career path starting with a small club of consultancies, auditors or banks before moving on to a corporation is a thing of the past. Today, companies look for the individual and their unique experiences, and although prior success can be a predictor of future success, organisations understand now that they need diversity of backgrounds, education and experience to compete in the global stage.

Carving your own path

What motivates you professionally? Position, power, curiosity, money, helping others, recognition? We all have different motivations during our lives, professional and personal, and typically several at once. For me, it was economic independence, curiosity and recognition, but above all, passion. Passion for life, for everything I do. Passion is the engine that affords me to enter into any new project with all my being. Passion is love, and love, we know, can move mountains. I have always been scared of mediocrity and sameness. I felt different growing up (don't we all?) and I wanted to succeed on my own terms. This was, and is, important for me: to carve my own path with my own failures and successes. I had an idea, a dream of what my future would look like, my instincts and my intuition, and a plan that would help me get there.

When I was young, there was conscription in Spain and I was sent to the island of Tenerife. I had never been to the Canary Islands before. It was far from my hometown of Gijón, Principado de Asturias, in the north of Spain. I really wanted to go to Madrid, the capital, so I could go to university, and being in Tenerife doing the menial tasks of a conscripted soldier did not appeal to me. It was going to be a year of boredom and a waste of time, so I had to do something about it. In the first two weeks of my stay there, several of the elite forces of Spain were actively recruiting for soldiers, from Green Berets to the Legion, but the one that caught my imagination was the Paratroopers Light Infantry Brigade. I could see myself learning new skills, combat and otherwise. It occurred to me that if I had to be drafted to the military, at least I should learn something new and useful, and jumping from planes felt new and fun. The spirit of adventure was inside of me and this promised to be one.

There were two things that sealed the deal for me: the Brigade was based in Alcalá de Henares in Madrid, and they paid you a small monthly stipend that would help with my desire for independence and self-reliance. However, you had to sign for two years rather than the one-year conscription. Given my instincts of where I wanted my life to go, it was a trade-off that I was willing to make. Before moving to Madrid, you had to do around three months of elite training in Alcantarilla, Murcia, where you learnt combat skills as well as jumping to obtain the title of 'cazador paracaidista' (roughly translated as 'paratrooper hunter'). The motto of the Paratroopers Brigade was 'Triunfar o Morir' ('Succeed or Die') and it was somewhat appropriate for my life journey in pursuit of success. (Not sure about the dying part, but as a youngster one gives in easily to flights of fancy and idealism!)

Looking back, I can see how my intuition was already directing me to the things that mattered to me, even though I was still too young to really be aware of that. Because of my passion for life, I took the challenge head-on and I did as much as I could to learn and grow while I was there. I loved skydiving from the start, but it was automatic parachute jumping where you are connected to a central line together with your fellow paratroopers, so I decided to keep training independently to learn proper manual skydiving and get the full experience and excitement of controlling the opening and the actual dive.

I still remember my first-ever army jump. We had been training for weeks, getting ready for that first jump. When the day finally came, we were all excited and ready for it.

The feeling I had as I pushed the plane off with my feet and took the plunge was one of madness and freedom. The parachute opened automatically and everything around me suddenly decelerated to slow-motion, as in a movie. I could see other fellow soldiers around me holding onto their parachute cords, slowly floating towards the earth. It was exhilarating and I remember shouting out loud: '*Qué huevos tengo!*' ('I've got big balls!'), but the shout also came out in slow motion, or so I remember it. It is difficult to describe it, but I felt that time had almost stopped around me. I have never experienced that since.

The earth came rushing to meet my feet, ending the slow-motion spell, and weeks of training took over, allowing me to roll over and absorb the impact. When I got up, I had a vivid thought in my head: 'If I have been able to overcome my fear and self-preservation instinct and jump from a plane, I can do anything in life.' I closed my eyes as I wanted to sear that moment into my brain forever. We all wanted to go for a second jump straight away, but we had to wait till the next day. I couldn't wait, I was so excited. I kept remembering that powerful feeling of strength, absolute freedom and no fear. I felt powerful, unique, indomitable and capable of anything. On our way back from the jump, all of us teenagers were shouting and laughing and sharing our unique but collective experience. The energy level was phenomenal. It was an adventure like no other, and each one of us was the hero of our own story. We were making history.

The next day could not come soon enough and we were all expectant and happy, ready to jump again. I remember getting up in the plane ready for the jump – the jump that I had been aching to do for the past twenty-four hours. I got to the door, and for a split second (that felt like minutes), my knees would not move. They were locked in place. My brain was sending the order to jump, but my body did not want to obey. It seemed that body memory and my secondary gut-brain were sending conflicting messages to my motor system, something like: 'Jumping from a plane is against nature and you could die, so I am protecting you and not letting you do this.' As I said, it was only a split second, but when you jump in the army, you are sharing the line with other soldiers and you cannot stop the motion. Once in the air, I felt great again, but conflicted. I wanted to jump more than anything, but my body did not want to. It was like I was not in charge of my own body for that moment in time. On that day, I understood what instinct really meant.

As we completed more dives over the following days, I never got that feeling again. Training took over and I focused on jumping better or landing this way or that way. I was learning; hence I was growing. I was happy. The powerful experience of my first two jumps has remained with me all my life. Every time I have felt conflicted or felt a fear of doing something, I remember how I overcame my natural instincts to do something somewhat unnatural, bold and daring. I was constructing the building blocks of my life: dream of a goal, pursue it to the fullest, master it, and move on to another in your overall quest for meaning and purpose. My own vision of success.

In your life you too have instincts, that gut feeling that compels you to do something. However, more often than not we repress our instincts because we may have a misconception of what is good or bad. We are perhaps trying to live up to someone else's expectations: family, friends, colleagues. We project other people's lives onto ours and that is a recipe for real failure. In your uniqueness, you must find your own path, your calling, what success looks like for you, and then pursue it with all your strength and passion. You will never go wrong if you follow your path. You be the judge of you. You do you.

If I had been able to overcome my fear and self-preservation instinct and jump from a plane, I could do anything in life.

Life is learning

As you design your career, like an architect building a beautiful and solid bridge, you will realise that as you experience new challenges, roles and projects, you acquire new elements to add to that design. Everything we do in life is a learning opportunity, and like the poem, it has no predetermined quality. It is neither good nor bad, it just is. If you look at life as a journey full of experiences, then you will recognise that everything is instructive, even the bad experiences. Pain is a vehicle of consciousness and it alerts us when something is not right. Through that pain, we learn to change, adapt, evolve. This is true of people and organisations alike. One of the most important lessons in your career is understanding that failure is part of success and to see the learning opportunity in it.

For most of my career I have worked internationally and have met many people from different backgrounds. This international life is part of my original vision and plan for life, as I always felt like a citizen of the world. It has always been an opportunity to learn about other cultures, different upbringing and circumstances and I truly enjoy making global friends. During one of my trips to Hong Kong, I met an unassuming man who ran a large company in South-East Asia. The company had been successful for a generation and he was proud of what he had created with his family. His beginnings were humble, but with his passion and determination he had made the company a national leader in its field. We were at dinner one night when he decided to confide in me about his company and his life. I pricked up my ears.

As a child he'd wanted to be a doctor, help people and travel, but soon learnt that it was something his family could not afford and he had to work from an early age to prosper. His future seemed predetermined to be one of hard work and hardships. As a teenager, he started to sell t-shirts that he and his sister designed at home. They manually painted white t-shirts with unique designs influenced by nature and animals in the wild that his sister created with flair. It was a manual endeavour that brought them a lot of joy, and also sustenance. They would sell a few t-shirts in the local market and go back home to produce more. Their t-shirts were quite unique and quirky and so they grew in popularity, allowing them to expand to other local markets.

The operation grew in no small part due to his passion for the business and his belief that they would be successful. They started to hire some friends and family to help with the business and bought printing and sewing machines to professionalise the process. They had to learn fast how to create a company and make it work, but they had no prior experience, so they hired a seasoned professional manager from the industry that was full of contacts, presence and ideas. Soon after, they were selling at a couple of major retailers in the territory and life seemed good. At this point he sighed and explained how, through his inexperience and naivety, the business was taken from under him by his manager, who quit the job and set up a parallel operation selling to the same retailers, but undercutting him in costs and distribution. As he had no patents or solid legal contracts with either the retailers or the manager, he was left with little, a huge sense of culpability for his company, his employees and his family and the inability to continue operations given the mounting costs and the lack of sales. He was devastated and distraught. He blamed himself for not paying attention to the basics and he had to let go of his staff and his entrepreneurial dream.

Most people would have complained to everyone who cared to listen about how unfair everything was, how they had been robbed, and tried to get the business back from the dreadful manager, but after the initial shock, he started thinking differently. He felt he had been taught a tough lesson, one he did not expect, and for a self-made man he wanted to make sure he thoroughly experienced the failure with all its pain and consequences, so he could move on the wiser. He did not want to forget it, but rather own it. As painful as it was, he saw it as a learning opportunity. Rather than wallowing in the loss, he started again, almost from scratch, but this time with a renewed determination to get it right. He was now going to create a business bigger and better. Three years later, he bought his old manager's business to add to his now dominant clothing and accessories business. He had grown way beyond his wildest expectations. His new organisation was much bigger, with hundreds of employees, international sales and a bright future. He told me he wasn't bitter when he bought out his old manager, and that during the sale, he took him aside and thanked him. His words were something like: 'Thank you for giving me the opportunity to learn what I needed to do to create what I have today. Thanks to you, I was able to understand my mistakes, pay attention to what was important and future-proof my vision for the company. Without you, I would have languished with a failed dream and would have spent my life complaining about what it could have been. Thank you.'

When he explained this to me, he did not sound triumphant or boasting. He was reflective and self-aware. He genuinely felt he had been given an opportunity to create something greater than himself and that his ex-employee was the catalyst and the tool for that learning and what came after it. This was his 'aha' moment, his learning inflection point, and he was really grateful for it. Pain had acted as a vehicle of consciousness for him, and created a pivotal moment in his life, not just his career. I was thoroughly impressed by his story and by the man himself.

One of the most important learnings in your career is understanding that failure is part of success and to see the learning opportunity in it.

How many times have you stopped and thought this way when something did not go the way you expected? When were you passed over for a promotion you really deserved or let go from a company without a valid reason? When things go wrong, when we 'fail', it is a subjective feeling. How you take that failure and make it into something positive, an inflection point in your career or your life, will determine who you are as an individual and what you will accomplish in life. Learning from your mistakes is the best way to combat them in the future and to turn something seemingly negative into the opposite.

As a leader, I deal with many different choices and changing circumstances, with successes and failures often at the same time. Nothing is linear. Trying to balance it all is not an easy task and you need clarity of mind, resolve and passion for what you do. Sometimes you go on your instincts, your intuition based on experience. Sometimes you follow the advice of people who know more than you about a particular issue or opportunity. What is important is to reflect on the problem and the potential solution and then act quickly. If you stop to think about how other people might view the outcome of your decisions, chances are that you will get a bout of paralysis and you'll do nothing. Sometimes inaction may be the right choice, but doing nothing because you fear failure is not a good reaction.

Being a leader means that you are expected to make decisions constantly. People will come to your door and expect you to drop everything and help them with their problems. They look at you as a purveyor of knowledge, solutions, and above all, decisions. People look for a clear framework to operate better, know their boundaries and take action, and in that framework, they need to have their manager, their leader, as the ultimate decision-maker, even if it is to back up their own conclusions.

He felt he had been taught a tough lesson, one he did not expect, and for a self-made man, he wanted to make sure he thoroughly experienced the failure with all its pain and consequences, so he could move on the wiser. He did not want to forget it, but rather own it.

Freedom to succeed

I remember when I worked for Grand Met in the nineties, there was a particular company value that has stuck with me since, and it is still visible on their website: 'We give ourselves and each other the *freedom to succeed*...'[19] As I recall, it meant to push you into action without fear of failure. Rather than using the expression 'freedom to fail', it was explained that failure was part of any future success as you tested, and tried, and kept trying until you got it right. What Grand Met wanted was action rather than inaction. The fear of failure is so irrational that it can stop people from making decisions and this can prevent the company from progressing.

While I worked at TripAdvisor, I remember a note that its founder and CEO, Steve Kaufer, had on his office door: *Speed Wins*. It was a neat phrase, short and to the point and quite typical of Steve's mind, a brilliant engineer. In my conversations with him, I understood that being fast did not mean to cut corners, but was an iterative process by which if something doesn't work, you change it immediately. Using this philosophy, it is possible to create a company culture where everyone can think fast and work fast without fear of failure. The issue in product-driven companies is that tasks can tend to expand to fill all the available time if you allow them. The faster you deliver a product to market, the faster you can add consumers to your product and then improve that product. Why go fast? Because the cost of failure is low in comparative terms, but the opportunity is great. This way, you can iterate your way to a large number of successes without fearing failure, but actually embracing it in the process.

---

19   'Who we are', Diageo.com. Available at: www.diageo.com/en/our-business/who-we-are

'Freedom to Succeed' and 'Speed Wins' are two principles that I have taken to heart and I have used them since, sharing them with my teams and companies as I have progressed in my career. The great thing about learning is that you can share it with other people; we are all both teachers and students, and this way we all advance. While you build your own career and path, remember the lessons, remember the failures as well as the successes. These will be gems in your backpack that will help you become who you want to be.

10

ONwards & UPwards

On my way to the top, I have gone through different evolutions, changing companies, jobs, functions, sectors and countries. I have tried many things, kept my vision at the centre of my plan and my passion as the driving engine of my 'Julio Project'. I have succeeded, failed, tried again and found new successes. I have laughed and cried, won and lost, and I have met incredible people along the way. To this day, I continue working with interesting people from different backgrounds that motivate and inspire me. It is like being a child again, a student of life. When in New York City, I walk around still looking upwards to the skyscrapers as if I am a tourist. I allow myself to enjoy things in life as if it were my first time. The ability to surprise yourself and not become jaded is essential to rekindle your passion for work and your passion for life.

Nowadays, I tend to work more with exciting startups where I invest, and with entrepreneurs, new and old, that seek my advice on strategy, expansion and growth. I like to share what I have learnt thus far while I continue learning every day. I discover new challenges constantly and try to resolve old and new problems as I push the organisation and the individuals forward. I keep enjoying what I do because I feel valued and needed; an important combination for everyone.

What I am not completely clear about is if I have really made it to 'the top', wherever that is. I suspect that I am still on my journey there. What I know is that I have made it to the top in one organisation both as Executive Chairman and CEO. Separately, as an investor and board director, I have arguably been (and am) at the top of different companies. But is that 'the top'? Conventional wisdom would probably concur that the CEO, as the head of the company, is at 'the top', but you also have investors, shareholders, the board of directors, the chairman of the board, all the governance and regulations of a listed company with audit and remuneration committees, nomination and compliance committees, a myriad of stakeholders, and not least of all, your employees. In other words, everyone has a boss. It never ends. Even when you are the boss of a company, you have a board that can ask you to leave, even though you may have been part of the nomination committee that put said directors in their position.

A popular example of this was Steve Jobs (RIP) who was forced out of Apple (a company he co-founded with Steve Wozniak in 1976) by the CEO and the board of directors with whom he disagreed. He came back years later as CEO and revolutionised the world we live in today. He was at 'the top' and one day he was thrown out of his own company, but as discussed in the prior chapter, he took that painful failure and turned it into a great and successful opportunity that ultimately gave us Pixar, NeXT and the new Apple company we know today valued at close to $3 trillion.

The ability to surprise yourself and not become jaded is essential to rekindle your passion for work and your passion for life.

Whose top is that?

I knew early on that I wanted to be the CEO, the boss, the número uno, or I at least wanted to be in a position to be able to choose, as my friend and mentor Ernest taught me early in my career. An American professor, he was interested in organisational behaviour and how hierarchical and non-hierarchical systems work within a company. He told me:

> 'What you see as an unreachable goal with the promise of economic freedom, power and influence may look different when you get there. The sacrifices you will need to make along the way may convince you that you don't want to be a CEO. You should put yourself in a position where you, and you alone, can choose. That is the real freedom: the opportunity to say no.'

I thought that this was powerful advice and I took it to heart. Now I see the fallacy of what being at the top really means. Yes, you may have decision-making power, money, influence and a fulfilling career, but what things have you sacrificed along the way? Relationships, family, stability, friends, hobbies, happiness perchance? It is all subjective and relative. If you commit your life to being an entrepreneur, a C-suite executive or a CEO, know that work becomes life, and life becomes work. They are one and the same. If you love what you do, then it does not feel like work. It is a continuum of your life, but the people around you are not 'on your trip'. It is lonely at the top and you need to prepare yourself for that. It is a personal journey. You are looking for that experience and using your passion and vision to get there, but it is for you and not those around you.

We all assume things about other people. When you are the boss, people will ascribe a number of qualities or defects to you as they experience you through their own lenses with their personal prejudices, fears and ambitions. This is something you cannot control, 'Oh Mighty Boss of company X.' For some, you will be a villain and for others, a saviour. Some will see you as the ideal ally for their careers, while others will see you as a hindrance to theirs. You will soon learn you can't win and that's OK.

As a leader, you will often feel vulnerable and you may have doubts about whether to show this or not. We have our own subjective views about how a leader should behave. These may be based on role models we have had, leaders we have read about, or even our parents. You will probably struggle choosing between how you want to behave at any given time and how you think you should behave. You cannot spend your time thinking about what other people think of you. You cannot measure yourself through the lens of somebody else, as this will stop you from being yourself.

Chief Servant Officer

Years ago, I gave an interview to BBC News where I shared some of my vulnerability and said that I wasn't really the Chief Executive Officer of the company, but rather the 'Chief Servant Officer'.[20] Some people may have taken it as false modesty, but to me it was a reflection of what the role of CEO really entails. Before I got to be the CEO, I thought that 'being the boss' would mean that I would make decisions and nobody would question me. I was obviously and painfully wrong: everyone questions you, from your employees to your board, and you need to have the answers (or at least know where to look for them). As the number one servant of the company, the expectation is that you will shepherd the company in the right direction. If you don't know how, you have no place at the top. The demands on you are important, and you must have broad shoulders and a willingness to listen, collaborate and direct at the same time.

Everyone wants your attention. In their minds, their issues or ideas are the most important and you are expected

---

20 Interview with Julio Bruno (2018) 'TimeOut boss: 'I am the chief servant officer', BBC News. Available at: www.bbc.co.uk/news/av/business-45512906

to drop everything and work on them immediately. You should also do this with a smile, even when you turn someone away. On many occasions, what they need is your acquiescence. You are the boss, so agreeing with their thinking is more important than anything else. It will empower them to continue working in that direction. If you don't agree, then you need to be a master persuader and show them a different way. Not a better way, just a different way that you believe is more suited to the current circumstances. In other words, you must be extremely good at communicating, persuading and bringing people along.

One thing I have learnt is that you need to listen much more than you ever thought you might. You are the leader, so in the eyes of your employees there is no need to 'prove yourself'. What they want is for you to know that they are also good at what they do. They need you to listen to and validate their thinking. A word of caution here: refrain from being their confessor or their psychoanalyst. This will rob you of your time and your objectivity, achieving little for either them or the company.

The demands on your time are endless when you are the CEO, so be careful how you spend it. Let's assume that your team is capable and what they really need from you is simply direction and encouragement. It sounds easy enough, but trust me, it isn't. As you grow in responsibilities, you may feel you know better, but there are many ways to resolve a problem. You may have a great idea, but it is not the only idea. Balancing the needs of the company and the individual are important, and as your duty is to be the best servant to the company, the one thing you need to learn is how to leave your ego at the door.

You cannot spend your time thinking about how other people think of you. You cannot measure yourself through the lens of somebody else as this will stop you from being yourself.

A friend of mine was CEO at a technology company. She had started as their product director and risen through the organisation. It had taken her many years of sacrifice to get there, and the day she got the final promotion, she was ecstatic. She felt that all her sacrifice had paid off with the culmination of her appointment as CEO. She soon learnt that the work had just started. With dwindling sales and loss of direction, the company needed a new focus. She needed to have a clear plan to move the company forward. She was a product expert with several stints in top tech companies globally, so there were few people with her knowledge and experience, but that was also her Achilles heel. She knew more than most people about product development, so it was difficult for her to empower someone to do her old job. Her new head of product could not do anything right in her book.

We were talking over coffee one day when she confided in me that she was having issues with product development. I listened carefully as she explained her frustrations. I added an occasional remark, but realised that I was just her sounding board. She already knew the solutions. My friend came to the conclusion that she was projecting her own insecurities on her new head of product and not letting go of her old job. We talked a bit more about the whole situation, but she had found the answer. She needed to not only empower him to do the job he was hired to do, but also listen to him and his new ideas, which would probably complement hers and be of additional value to the company. It wasn't that anything was wrong with either of their views, just that you need to allow other people to flourish and bring a new perspective to the role. As a leader, she realised that this was part of her job. By serving him, she was serving the company. She paid for the coffee.

It is lonely at the top

As you become the leader of your department, division or corporation, you will increasingly feel a bit detached and somewhat excluded from the rest of the company, and yes, you will feel alone. No whining here; it is part of the burden of being the leader. Five years after taking over from Steve Jobs, CEO of Apple, Tim Cook, told *The Washington Post,* 'It's sort of a lonely job. The adage that it's lonely – the CEO job is lonely – is accurate in a lot of ways. I'm not looking for any sympathy.'[21] Yes, it is a lonely job, but you have chosen it. You agreed to do this job, just be aware of what it means, for better and for worse. The

---

21   J McGregor (2016) 'Tim Cook the interview: Running Apple "is sort of a lonely job"', *The Washington Post.* Available at: www.washingtonpost.com/sf/business/2016/08/13/tim-cook-the-interview-running-apple-is-sort-of-a-lonely-job

expectations put upon you are plenty, but the rewards for success are plentiful too.

At the so-called top, you will learn that most people don't care, or don't have the time to care, about your wellbeing. You are there to serve them, and in general, people will not be thinking about you. That is your job: to think about them and their welfare. I don't wish to play the world's smallest violin, but be aware that because you are the boss, you are expected to worry about everyone else and not the other way around.

Despite all of this, it does have its rewards. In the same interview I referred to earlier, when asked about his tenure as CEO, Tim Cook said,

> 'I've got the best job in the world. I think about my day and weeks and months and years – I put them in three buckets: people, strategy and execution… I always think the most important one of those is people. If you don't get that one right, it doesn't matter what kind of energy you have in the other two – it's not enough.'

There you have it, from one of the best CEOs in the world, lonely or not, warts and all, he feels he has the best job in the world. I'm not going to compare my tenure as CEO with that of Tim Cook, running one of the largest and most successful companies in the world, but I agree with him. I also felt that I had the best job in the world. Despite the scrutiny, the loneliness and the demands placed on you and your time, being the CEO allowed me to fulfil part of my plan, the original vision of that ambitious young man of all those years ago.

It also allowed me to grow as an individual, serve people and help others grow, and fight together for the wellbeing and the future of the company and its employees. We were doing something great together, we were on a mission, and that is a powerful feeling. It also helped me learn more about myself, who I was as a leader and as a person, what I enjoyed and what I did not. It opened my eyes about the realities of corporate life at the highest level and I am only grateful for the opportunity. It is a relatively small 'club' and I enjoy being a member. It allowed me to meet people and places that perhaps I could have not done otherwise.

I don't wish to play the world's smallest violin, but be aware that because you are the boss, you are expected to worry about everyone else, and not the other way around.

Walk the walk, talk the talk

When I was coming up in the business world, an older manager told me, 'You must look the part to be the part.' I remember thinking that this was far too simple and obvious. At the time, everyone wore suits and ties to the office (today that feels like something out of a movie), so if you were an office worker you were already 'looking the part'. On reflection, I understand what he meant. Looking the part was also acting the part (as we discussed in Chapter 6) and behaving as if you were already there. This means thinking like a good boss would think, pre-empting issues before they occur and looking further into the future to move forward more efficiently. It also means the way you behave, how you relate to others, conduct yourself in meetings and your overall demeanour. Are you there to contribute and be part of your company long term, or are you just a tourist?

As I grew through the ranks, I also learnt that your face gives out clues to people about you, and the higher you get in a company, the more important it is that you are aware of this. Oftentimes somebody would approach me, and to my bewilderment, they would ask me, 'What's the matter?' I wouldn't understand the question. I'd perhaps been deep in thought about something or preoccupied with something at home, but it had nothing to do with work. The higher you are in an organisation, the more careful you need to be with your visual clues. Your colleagues, and employees in general, are scanning your face for answers about the future of the company, and ultimately, their jobs. They read into everything even when there is nothing to read, so you must look the part and have a cordial outlook that doesn't show more than is needed. I'm not saying you have to be a robot, just that you must have your poker face on more often than not. People need reassurance and if, say, your company is going through transformation, people will look for clues everywhere. My advice is to smile as often as you can and never lose your composure.

Passionate leadership

Today, as I work with other leaders, entrepreneurs and corporations, I feel I am a more rounded leader. By helping others achieve their goals and their visions, I am, in effect, helping myself to fulfil more of mine. My work still affords me to travel the world and get involved in many different, interesting projects and opportunities. My experience is a valuable asset for companies and other people, and I enjoy sharing what I know, while I continue learning in the process. The vision is the same, but the plan has evolved. I believe it will continue to evolve and mutate until the day I die.

Being a leader is a journey. I don't believe in natural-born leaders, but on made leaders. You can have natural abilities to become a leader, but you need so much more than natural predisposition. You must want to be a leader and be prepared to learn and grow every day. Motivating and inspiring others does not come easily to anyone, I believe.

What are some of the key qualities and characteristics that define a leader? You must:

- Believe in yourself.

- Be vulnerable and strong in equal measure.

- Be curious and eager to learn constantly from everybody, everything, everywhere.

- Be honest with yourself and others and be transparent in your interactions. Use your emotional intelligence.

- Be firm and be guided by values. Don't procrastinate.

- Have a clear vision of what you want to achieve, a plan, and the drive to get there.

- Inspire and motivate people with your vision and your passion and empower others. Be an evangelist of the company and its mission.

- Make sure your company reflects society in all its diversity. Great talent is everywhere. Don't miss out.

- Be passionate about everything you do.

Passion is the key. Without passion, we just go through the motions, with the current, rather than writing our own destiny. You want to feel the blood running through your veins, following your dream and making that dream collective. You should aspire to infecting other people with your vision and your passion, bringing the best out of people and sharing in a journey where everyone will learn their measure. We are all at different stages in our careers and our lives, but great leaders inspire us to do better, to be better.

I'm in my life journey and I am still making the path as I walk. What I have learnt thus far is helping me to take the next step. The vision that brought me here is still part of who I am, who I have become. My path is the journey. I hope that my thoughts and experiences help you find your path, too. Remember, passion is the key; the key is passion.

Acknowledgements

There are many people that have, in some way or another, helped me in my life and my career and have contributed somehow to the essence of this book, but I cannot acknowledge all of them, even if my memory allowed it.

I dedicate this book to my father (RIP), who loved me and inspired me and made me see the value of being a jack-of-all-trades, a true Renaissance man. I miss him. And to my mother, my first entrepreneur role model. I love you.

My sisters Angeles, Isabel, Natividad and Henar, and my brother Antonio, who continue to be my source of love and inspiration. I can always count on you. My nephews, nieces and the rest of my extended family. I love you.

I have been grateful throughout my life for people who have helped me be better than I am and have pushed me in the right direction, whether they were aware of it or not. Manuel G. Anuarbe, my first mentor and guide, who helped me see what it could be. Don Manuel Morán (RIP), my first schoolteacher, for inspiring me as a child to believe in myself and always use the power of my imagination. Ernest, who taught me the power of education and perseverance. Noel Caro, for being the friend that always believes in you, no matter what. I love you. Carlos Galdón, for inspiring me to try new horizons.

My colleagues, clients and friends at Time Out, TripAdvisor, Belly, Travelport, Regus, Energizer, Diageo, Hola!, Floe, Audicus, Flyt, Roasting Plant, CoverWallet, Mercato Metropolitano, Cervantes Theatre, and all the companies and startups that I have been involved with, past and present. You know who you are. I thank you all.

Iñaki Berenguer, a friend and serial entrepreneur, who showed me the value of disruption.

Euprepio Padula, a friend who showed me the value of reinvention.

Mark Dixon, who showed me the value of grit and never giving up.

Eduardo Sánchez and Javier Junco who showed me the value of kindness at work.

Kym Edwards, 'because you can never have enough good people'.

Steve Kaufer, because 'speed wins'.

Peter Dubens, for giving me the opportunity to lead Time Out.

Tony Elliott (RIP), a great entrepreneur and media visionary. You are missed.

I would like to thank José Pascual Marco, Caroline McGuinn, Paul Blanchard, Luis Lain and Cristiana Cau for their advice and thoughtful feedback for this book, as well as Mindy Gibbins-Klein for motivating me to keep writing and be candid about my life experiences.

Thank you all!